D0539671

Revise
OPENING WORLDS
& OPENING LINES

Michele Paule

Steve Cooper **(Experienced examiner)**

Heinemann

Inspiring generations

Heinemann is an imprint of Pearson Education Limited,
a company incorporated in England and Wales, having
its registered office at Edinburgh Gate, Harlow, Essex,
CM20 2JE. Registered company number: 872828

Heinemann is a registered trademark of
Pearson Education Limited

First published 2003

10
10 9 8

British Library Cataloguing in Publication Data is available
from the British Library on request.

ISBN 978 0 435150 96 9

Designed by Jackie Hill, 320 Design
Produced by AMR Ltd

Cover design by hicksdesign

Cover photographs: Eye Ubiquitous (woman); Getty (red leaves)

Cover quotations: extract from 'Imitations' by Dannie Abse © Dannie Abse, published by
Hutchinson, reprinted with permission of The Peters Fraser and Dunlop Group Limited
and extract from 'Mort aux Chats' by Peter Porter © Peter Porter, reprinted with kind
permission of the author.

Permissions sought by Jackie Newman

Picture research by Kay Altwegg

The publishers would like to thank the following for permission to reproduce
photographs on the pages noted: Photodisc (stack of books), pp.4–13; Photodisc (man
and woman), pp.15–17; Photodisc (tree), pp.18–20; Photodisc (mother and child),
pp.21–3; Source unknown (trenches), pp.24–6; Photodisc (stack of books), pp.27–45;
Illustrated London News (war veteran), pp.47–9; Rural History Centre, University of
Reading (harvester), pp.50–3; Peter Morris (mirrored face), pp.54–6; Source Unknown
(soldiers), pp.57–9; Photodisc (stack of books), pp.60–80; Camera Press/Miriam Berkley
(Achebe), pp.81–2; Camera Press (Head), pp.83–4; Camera Press/John Reardon
(Gordimer), pp.85–6; Art & Culture Magazine, Matichon Group, Thailand (Srinawk),
pp.87–8; AP (Tan), pp.89–90; Enorth.co.cn Tianjin Enorth Net News Co. Ltd. (Ji-Cai),
pp.91–2; Trevor Seely (Seely), pp.93–4; Peepal tree Press (Khan), pp.95–6; Camera
Press/Jane Bown (Jhabvala), pp.97–8; Shiel Land Associates/AP Photos (Narayan),
pp.99–100; Camera Press (Desai), pp.101–2; Camera Press (Nagibin), pp.103–4;
Photodisc (stack of books) pp.105–27.

The publishers would also like to thank Anna Gregory and Joe Swarbrick for their kind
contributions.

Printed in China(CTPS/08)

CONTENTS

HOW TO ACHIEVE SUCCESS

OPENING LINES
poetry past and present
2003-2008

OPENING WORLDS
short stories from different cultures
2003-2008*

* subject to availability

Introduction

How to use this revision guide

This book will help support your revision of the OCR poetry and short story collections – **Opening Lines** and **Opening Worlds** – in the final few months of your GCSE English and English Literature courses. You can work through it on your own, but it will also be helpful in a group or class context. The book provides:

- ✔ general advice about revision techniques
- ✔ activities to help you revise the poetry and the stories in detail
- ✔ strategies for linking and pairing poems and stories
- ✔ practice with exam questions
- ✔ sample answers with examiner comments
- ✔ advice on question choice
- ✔ advice on time management, and planning and checking exam answers
- ✔ advice on writing exam answers, including using quotations and comparisons.

How the collections fit into your courses

The two collections can be used in a number of different ways in each of your English courses. It all depends on your choices and particularly on which English Literature course you choose to follow (Scheme A: Units 1–4; Scheme B: Units 5–8), but it's possible for you to cover 60% of your English Literature course and 15% of your English course with work based on these two texts alone.

OPENING LINES (poetry)	OPENING WORLDS (short stories)
English:	**English:**
Coursework, Unit 4 Literary Heritage = 5% OR	Exam, Unit 2 Different Cultures = 10% (35 minutes on one question chosen from two alternatives, covering two stories)
Exam, Unit 3 Literary Heritiage = 5% (30 minutes on one question chosen from two alternatives, covering two poems)	
English Literature:	**English Literature:**
Exam, Units 2 or 6 Poetry = 25% (45 minutes on one question chosen from three alternatives, covering two poems)	Exam, Unit 2 Prose = 25% (45 minutes on one question chosen from three alternatives, covering two stories)
Coursework, Units 3 or 7 Prose = 10% OR	Coursework, Unit 7 Prose = 10% OR
Exam, Units 4 or 8 Prose = 10% (30 minutes on one question chosen from two alternatives, covering two poems)	Exam, Unit 8 Prose = 10% (30 minutes on one question from two alternatives, covering two stories)

English Literature

In **Scheme A**, 70% of your marks will come from exam work on Post-1914 texts and 30% from coursework on Pre-1914 texts. You can choose to study one of the

Post-1914 sections in **Opening Lines** as your poetry text for the exam and the twelve stories in **Opening Worlds** as your prose text. You can also use some Pre-1914 poems from **Opening Lines** for your coursework (or the exam alternative).

In **Scheme B**, 70% of your marks will come from exam work on Pre-1914 texts and 30% for coursework on Post-1914 texts. You can choose a Pre-1914 section from **Opening Lines** as your poetry text for the exam and some of its Post-1914 poems for your coursework (or the exam alternative). Because the **Opening Worlds** stories are all Post-1914, you can only use them for coursework (or the exam alternative).

English

You have to write about poetry as part of the reading requirement for your coursework (Unit 4) or for the exam alternative (Unit 3). You can choose to use any of the Post-1914 poets (or the Pre-1914 poets marked NC) in **Opening Lines** for coursework. You can choose to study **Opening Worlds** as your prose text for the Different Cultures exam (Unit 2); only six of the stories will be set for this exam.

Making sense of the Assessment Objectives

The Assessment Objectives sum up what you have to do to succeed in English and English Literature. The examiners keep them in mind as they mark your work.

English Literature

Your work on the two collections will help you to achieve all of the Assessment Objectives for English Literature, which are as follows:

1. **Respond to texts critically, sensitively and in detail, selecting appropriate ways to convey your response, using textual evidence as appropriate.** Show that you know the texts well, that you have thought about them and can support your ideas and insights with direct quotation and other textual references. You can also express your responses to the texts in a clear, organised and detailed way.

2. **Explore how language, structure and forms contribute to the meaning of texts, considering different approaches to texts and alternative interpretations.** Show awareness of the way in which a text is written rather than just concentrating on content (the '*how* is it written' rather than '*what* is it about' approach). This awareness of the choices that a writer makes to convey a range of meanings and to achieve a range of effects is a key element in achieving high marks.

3. **Explore relationships between texts, selecting and evaluating relevant material.** Show that you can compare texts, looking closely at links and contrasts, similarities and differences. Your work on pairs of poems from **Opening Lines** could be central to achieving this objective, both in your exams and your coursework.

4. **Relate texts to their social, cultural and historical contexts and literary traditions.** All the exam questions on **Opening Worlds** and other prose texts will enable you to show awareness of the context of a particular story or novel. You may be asked to explore the presentation of particular attitudes and beliefs in the texts, for example, or to focus on the reasons for social or personal conflict. The *contextual*, like the *comparative*, requirement is a compulsory element for your exams and your coursework, and the twelve stories in **Opening Worlds**, from a wide range of cultures, could be central to achieving this objective.

Stories set for your examination year:

June 2003–January 2006
• Dead Men's Path
• Snapshots of a Wedding
• The Train from Rhodesia
• The Gold-Legged Frog
• Two Kinds
• The Tall Woman and Her Short Husband

June 2006–January 2008*
• The Pieces of Silver
• The Red Ball
• The Young Couple
• Leela's Friend
• Games at Twilight
• The Winter Oak

subject to availability

English

Work on the two collections will also help you to achieve two of the key Assessment Objectives for English, which are very similar to Objectives 1 and 2 for English Literature.

1 Read with insight and engagement, making appropriate references to text and developing and sustaining interpretations of them.

2 Understand and evaluate how writers use linguistic, structural and presentational devices to achieve their effects, and comment on ways language changes and varies.

Exam questions

Regardless of which exam they are in, the questions on poetry will be similar in style. However, they will be adapted to fit the different time limits: 30 minutes in English, Unit 3; 45 minutes in English Literature, Units 2 and 6; and 30 minutes in English Literature, Units 4 and 8.

The same is true for the questions on stories: 35 minutes in English, Unit 2; 45 minutes in English Literature, Unit 2; and 30 minutes in English Literature Unit 8.

Most of the advice in this book is designed to help you with the questions on the longer papers (English Literature, Units 2 and 6) which are worth the most marks. Nevertheless, as long as you keep an eye on the different timings, the advice will help you with all the Units in which the two collections appear.

What the examiners are looking for

✔ Relevance – you must answer the question they have set and show awareness of the links between the poems or stories in the question.

✔ Response – you must express your view of the poems or stories in relation to the question.

✔ Textual detail – you must support your response with direct quotation and with detail from the poems or stories.

✔ Evaluation – you must look closely at how the poems or stories are written.

✔ Expression – you must make sure that you express your ideas clearly and accurately. In English Literature, for example, 5% of your marks will depend on your control of spelling, punctuation and sentence structure.

Annotation

From June 2005 there is a rule change for the exam. You will not be allowed to write notes in the texts that you take with you into the exams. A lot of notes written in the margin can sometimes stop you from expressing your own ideas or distract you from answering the question directly. So, for the exams from June 2005 onwards, you will be supplied with working copies of both **Opening Lines** and **Opening Worlds**, which you can annotate as you wish throughout the course, and then you will be given clean copies for use in the exams.

An examination answer might use the Three-part formula.

Three-point formula
• **Respond** (make a relevant point)
• **Quote** (support the point with a quotation from the text)
• **Comment** (evaluate the effect of the writing in the quotation)

Active revision

Active revision is good for you ... and for your results! Did you know that we remember only: 5% of what we hear, but 40% of what we discuss; 10% of what we read, but 60% of what we actively do and 90% of what we teach others.

Reading through the texts and your notes will help you remember the content and ideas, but you need to be confident of your skills too. In the exam you will need to:

✔ think on your feet
✔ explore ideas about and connections between texts
✔ support and develop your points through quotation and discussion of effects
✔ structure your answer.

Don't worry. You can practise the skills you need to get the best possible grade in the examination, as well as revise the text. There are lots of ideas to help you on the following pages in this section and you'll find more examples of how the techniques work in the sections on the poetry and the stories, and in the sample questions.

Reading and thinking

These activities will help you to:
✔ check your knowledge and understanding of the texts
✔ increase your familiarity with key features of the texts
✔ discuss and explain your ideas about the texts
✔ identify any areas you may feel less sure about.

Reading and thinking on your own

1 Do this activity on your own or in class. Gather together your annotated texts, copies of the texts with no annotations and your exercise book or class notes from your original study of the texts.

2 Choose a poem or story and read through a copy with no annotations.

3 Make a note of the following points:

Poems	Stories
• what it is about	• what it is about
• key mood or emotions	• key or dramatic events
• interesting and/or effective words and phrases	• opening and ending
• pace and rhythm and their effect	• key features of character and/or setting
• structure.	• narrative voice.

4 Compare your ideas with your class notes or your annotated version. Did you cover the important ideas? Did you spot anything new?

The pairs game

When you have looked at all the poems in your Section, create categories for pairing based on your notes. You could:

- identify two poems with interesting structures
- find two poems with contrasting views on the same subject
- find two stories with a strong sense of place or striking imagery
- find two stories where a character learns something.

When you have done this, try to add more poems or stories to make groups of three or four. Then compare your pairs or groups with a partner's.

Reading, thinking and discussing

1. In pairs or groups agree who will take notes and feed back to the class. Gather a copy each of the texts in your Section, and paper and pens.

2. Choose one text each. Create some questions about your text trying to cover key areas such as subject, mood and language; imagery, structure (for poetry) and character; setting, drama and mood (for stories).

3. Swap texts and questions. Through discussion, answer the questions you have been given. Explain your answers as fully as you can.

4. Ask your partner or other group members if they have anything to add to your answers.

5. After you have all had the chance to discuss each text, make a note of any problem areas or difficult questions. Discuss these with your teacher or the whole class.

Using more brain power and making connections

These activities will help you to:
- ✔ increase your learning through using more of your brain – here you will use visual sense and hearing
- ✔ create a revision resource which highlights language effects
- ✔ think about texts from different angles
- ✔ make links and comparisons between different texts.

Using your ears

1. Gather a tape recorder and tape, and find a quiet place to record.

2. Read though the texts and decide the following:
   - how quickly or slowly they should be read
   - what tone of voice or emotion is needed – and if, when and how it changes
   - where to pause and where to run on for dramatic effect.

3. When you feel confident, read the texts aloud for the recording, trying to:
   - emphasise pace and rhythm
   - change the tone of your voice to fit the emotion, speaker, dialogue, atmosphere
   - follow the punctuation rather than the line pattern in poems to emphasise the flow and/or pauses
   - exaggerate the different features and/or effects to highlight them.

Top tip

Use your recording on a personal stereo to revise while you are doing other things, such as washing the dishes.

Brainstorming

A brainstorm helps you to explore an individual subject or poem in detail, generate ideas, remember details and focus, select and order information. It is often the first stage of mindmapping, but can also be done independently.

1 Study the example of a brainstorm below.

2 Create a brainstorm on a poem you will be revising for the exam. Include all the important details you can think of.

3 Decide on the order in which you would cover these ideas in the exam. Number the branches of your brainstorm. Look at how a structure is becoming clear.

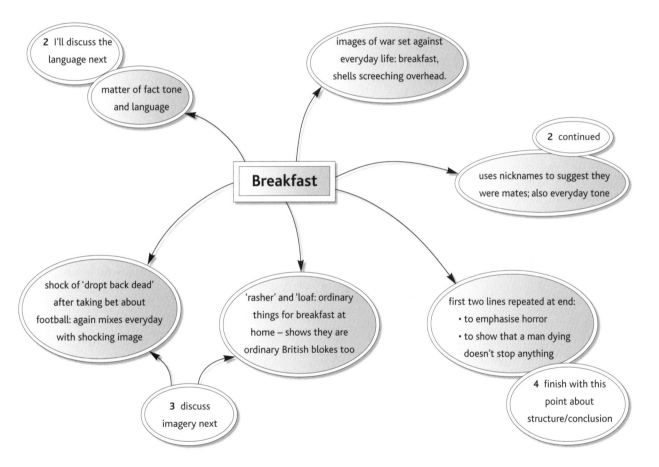

2 I'll discuss the language next

matter of fact tone and language

images of war set against everyday life: breakfast, shells screeching overhead.

Breakfast

2 continued

uses nicknames to suggest they were mates; also everyday tone

shock of 'dropt back dead' after taking bet about football: again mixes everyday with shocking image

'rasher' and 'loaf: ordinary things for breakfast at home – shows they are ordinary British blokes too

first two lines repeated at end:
• to emphasise horror
• to show that a man dying doesn't stop anything

3 discuss imagery next

4 finish with this point about structure/conclusion

Mindmapping

In mindmaps the ideas also spread out from a central point, but they allow you to extend ideas with examples and comments. Mindmapping is a technique for getting more of your brain to think and learn. You can use colour, the space on the page and images, and these help more. Mindmaps will help you to:

✔ link ideas together
✔ explore connections between poems
✔ learn more quickly so you don't need to spend so much time going over things
✔ think more efficiently
✔ plan answers with important ideas that are organised well.

Creating icon images to represent themes

The following activity will help you to:

✔ create memorable visual images to help you remember ideas
✔ practise thinking around the three-point formula
✔ get your ideas into order before writing
✔ explore poems from unusual angles and investigate new links.

1 Create a list of the key themes or ideas in your Section.

2 Create or download a small, simple image to represent each theme. You could also use customised stamps or stickers, if they are small enough.

3 Add images to the corners of pages of your exercise book or your copy of **Opening Lines** to remind you which poems deal with which key themes and ideas.

Creating a mindmap

1 Study the example of a mindmap below, which explores the different aspects of a theme in a range of poems.

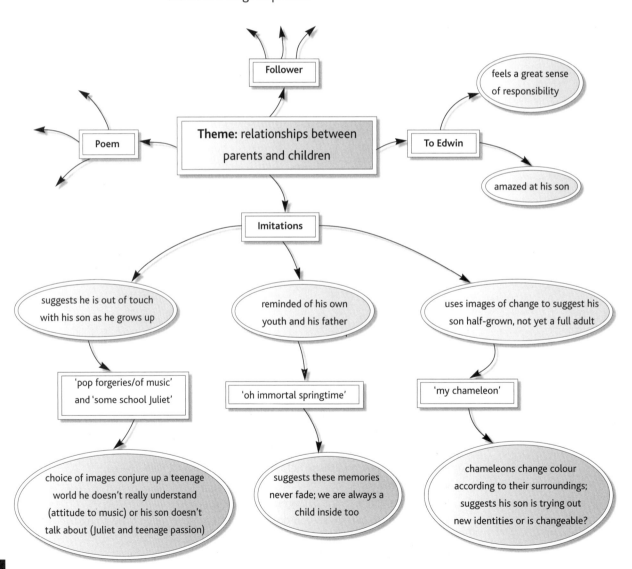

2. Choose a key theme from your Section.

3. Create a similar mindmap on a large sheet of paper using plenty of coloured pens or pencils (even though the example here has to be in black and white). Add suitable symbols to represent the ideas.

4. Extend each branch with quotation and explanations (even though we have not had enough space to extend all the branches in the example).

Concept mapping

A concept map is a visual aid like a mind map, but instead of exploring different aspects of one subject, it helps you explore different links between more than one subject.

Creating a concept map

1. Gather together a copy of the texts, a large piece of paper and pens or pencils in different colours.

2. Identify the key ideas or themes from the texts in your section and choose a different colour for each key theme.

3. Write the text titles you are studying on the paper, making sure they are roughly the same distance from each other.

4. For each key theme, draw theme lines in the chosen colours connecting the relevant texts. Write along the theme line in the same colour, explaining why you have linked the texts in this way.

Here is an example of a concept map on creatures.

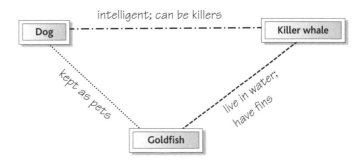

Once you've revised the texts and got the skills at your fingertips, you'll be well underway to preventing any last minute panics, but the next section gives you a few tips on panic busting too.

Panic busters

HOW TO ACHIEVE SUCCESS

Here is a student's piece of writing about sitting an English Literature exam. Look for the tips you can use to prepare yourself and tackle the exam.

A full 20 minutes early, the hall has already attracted a large crowd of very nervous students.

These are the people with highly organised, coloured-in revision timetables pinned to their walls like mission briefings in a war film. They imagine a rather fierce general barks orders to re-read texts, study revision guides, make tapes of notes, get plenty of sleep ...

They quiz each other with quick-fire questions on onomatopoeia and why most of the characters in 'Of Mice and Men' begin with the letter C. Crazy theories are flung around, adding to the tension. It is wise in a situation like this to avoid everyone. I only know what I know. I cannot change what is now in my head.

Open your papers. Now ...

I flick to the correct section, wasting no time. The question is good. Calm but quick, the essay is planned with scribbles and underlining, annotations of the texts are read, re-read, processed and contextualised.

Exactly how to write a good exam essay has become natural. Five lines of introduction are proceeded by three healthy 15-line paragraphs and a neat double bow of a conclusion. Right on schedule, the essay is finished. Nothing can go wrong now. What's next?

Don't panic. Just re-read the question. No no no. I didn't revise that poem. I have no annotations. Instead of making me want to weep, this fuels me with competitiveness. I shall answer this question!

Unfortunately, this has left me with 3/4 of an hour to answer my final question. Confidently, the introduction is as short and to the point as a bullet. Slowly, my handwriting is becoming more muddled, as is the complexity of my analysis. Big words instead of small. The paragraphs are shorter. Yet somewhere in my head a voice whispers a comforting mantra of Respond – Quote - Comment, which keeps the structure of my otherwise wild paragraphs in line. Five minutes left. Points left sloppily dragging are hastily double-knotted in a four line conclusion, bringing the essay to a sharp close. A quick check for spelling, grammar and punctuation and it is over.

Be able to use technical terms and discuss their effects.

Be confident about your revision. Don't try to absorb last minute ideas.

Annotation is for highlighting key features – not making notes to copy.

Structure is important: introduce ideas, explore them in clear paragraphs; then sum up.

Read a difficult question again. Don't forget you have a choice.

Use simple language and structures. Unnecessary complications don't impress. Use technical terms as tools.

Any of these tactics help you?

Don't worry about different ideas from your own – there's a range of valid ones.

A plan is key to help organise thoughts and build an outline of points. It needn't be neat.

Be confident – practise skills such as planning and writing essays as well as revising texts.

Timing is crucial – don't leave too little for the next part.

Revise them all – the exam won't focus only on the ones you like.

A good introduction clearly and briefly sets out your approach.

Structuring writing must be second nature to help keep ideas in order and show you can explore and discuss effects.

Leave time to check for unnecessary mistakes at the end.

Top tips for preparation

✔ Revise the texts, including your ideas on them and the vocabulary used in them. The best way to do this is by practising your skills of thinking and writing about the texts.

✔ Practise structuring your essays by:
  - finding and analysing key words and phrases
  - creating Respond – Quote – Comment puzzles with friends
  - making quick plans for a range of questions.

✔ Create opportunities for timing your work. How much can you write? How long do you need for planning and checking?

Top tips for the exam

✔ Stick to a time plan for each question. Allow about a third of your time for reading, planning and checking through, for example 10 minutes for reading and planning, 30 minutes for writing and 5 minutes for checking.

✔ Highlight the key words in the question and use them regularly in your answer.

✔ Watch out for two- and even three-part questions. Make sure that you cover all the parts of the question and both of the poems or stories evenly.

✔ Brainstorm a few ideas. Plan them into some kind of paragraph order and pick out some relevant details from the text, before you start writing your answer.

✔ Start each paragraph with an idea that clearly relates to the question.

✔ As you write, keep asking: Am I answering the question? What relevant response am I expressing? What textual evidence am I using to support this response?

✔ Use the three-point formula: Respond – Quote – Comment.

✔ Use brief quotations which fit neatly into your sentences.

✔ Use the writer's name and try to focus on the choices that the writer makes – the *how* as well as the *what*!

✔ Show your awareness of different possible interpretations. Use expressions like: 'however', 'although', 'on the other hand', 'perhaps', 'this could suggest' and 'this could express'.

✔ Save a fresh point for your final paragraph so that your conclusion doesn't just sum up and repeat what you have already said. A point about how the stories or the poems end, if it relates to the question, is often a good way to finish.

✔ Check the spelling of the writers' and characters' names. Don't get them wrong.

Remember that there is no such thing as a perfect answer to questions on literature texts. The examiners will not have a rigid mark scheme or a model answer to set your answers against. They genuinely want to know what you think, so don't trot out other people's ideas especially if you don't understand them properly. The questions are addressed to you as an individual with your own views and the examiners are hoping for a personal response grounded in the text.

Good luck!

Poetry for examination in 2003–2006

Men and Women

Confidence checklist

In a chart like the one below, place a tick in the appropriate column for each statement depending on how confident you feel.

Statement	Not confident	Could do more work	Very confident
I can compare two poems that show different attitudes to love.			
I can explore the way women are shown in at least two poems.			
I can explore the different ways in which love is expressed in the poems.			
I can discuss two poems that show a negative side of love.			
I can identify which poems are sonnets and discuss their features.			
I can discuss interesting imagery in a range of poems.			
I can explore the ways in which attitudes to men, women and love have changed or stayed the same over time.			

Re-read the poems that need more work, with your notes, highlighting what you don't understand. Discuss them with a partner or ask your teacher for help.

Memory joggers

This quiz will help you to:
✔ test your memory of the texts and their content
✔ identify which poems you may still need to work on
✔ think quickly and recall key details.

1 In which poem does the poet know his love is lying to him? Why doesn't he mind?

2 Who would rather be forgotten than remembered with sadness?

3 Who dreams of peace and solitude? Identify four different images taken from nature that show this.

4 Whose clothes does her lover find exciting? What are the clothes made of?

5 Who pretends to be glad about a break-up? What image of the end of love does he create?

6 Who tries to frighten his lover into bed with descriptions of the grave? Why?

7 In which poem are women warned against marriage? For what reasons?

8 In which poem does an immoral woman have a better life than her virtuous friend? What is the immoral woman's name? Identify three ways in which her life is better than before.

9 What does the walk of a stranger remind Amy Levy of?

10 Who likens his past loves to wild birds that used to be tame? How does he account for this behaviour?

11 What colour does Thomas Hardy's young woman wear to say goodbye?

12 In which poem does the lover feel like a prince?

When you have finished, check your answers with your teacher or against the poems and make a note of which poems you think you need to work on more.

Thinking and linking

Exam questions will ask you to write about common themes or ideas in the poems. This activity will help you to think about the ways in which poems can be linked or grouped together.

1 Copy and complete the chart below to show which poems, in your opinion, contain the listed themes or ideas. The first one has been done for you.

2 Add other themes, e.g. 'Men in love' and 'Seduction', and complete these rows too.

Theme	Poems		
The end of love	'Since there's no help ...'	'Remember'	'They flee from me ...'
Ways of expressing love			
Women in love			
Marriage/the alternative			
Appearance and reality			
Love and death			

3 For each poem you have chosen, select at least three quotations that help convey the theme or idea.

4 For each quotation, add notes explaining how it helps to convey the theme or idea. For example:

Poem: 'Since there's no help ...'

Quotation: Showing the end of love – 'his pulse failing, Passion speechless lies,/ ... bed of death'.

Explanation: the poet describes love like a man on his death bed with life ebbing out of him. This technique is called personification.

Extension

Choose one of the examples. Create at least three more sets of boxes on that poem alone, choosing different points and examples for each box.

Thinking and writing

This activity will help you to:
- ✔ practise locating key details in the poems – finding the words that do the work
- ✔ comment closely on language features
- ✔ reinforce a useful approach to paragraph structure.

The example below is given as a three-point formula. You should try to follow this pattern. Fill in the missing part(s) for each of the other poems in the chart.

The Ruined Maid

Respond → In 'The Ruined Maid', one of the ways Hardy suggests that the 'ruined' girl's life is much better is through her clothes.

Quote → Melia's friend remembers that she 'left us in tatters, without shoes or socks' but now has 'gay bracelets and bright feathers three'.

Comment → This contrast shows that before she did not even have the basics, whereas now she can afford luxurious accessories.

A Woman Is a Worthy Thing

Respond →

Quote → He describes how women 'do the wash and do the wring'.

Comment → The repetition in the structure of this line reinforces the repetitive daily chores that make up women's lives.

To His Coy Mistress

Respond → In 'To His Coy Mistress', Marvell mocks his lover's reluctance.

Quote → He tells her that if they had the time, 'An hundred years should go to praise/Thine eyes'.

Comment →

A Scherzo – A Shy Person's Wishes

Respond → Dora Greenwell uses images of small, hidden things in nature to show how she longs to hide from the world. An example of this is …

Quote →

Comment →

On the Departure Platform

Respond →

Quote → 'and moment by moment got/Smaller and smaller'.

Comment →

Time and Change

Confidence checklist

In a chart like the one below, place a tick in the appropriate column for each statement depending on how confident you feel.

Statement	Not confident	Could do more work	Very confident
I can compare two poems that suggest childhood is the best time of life.			
I can identify and explore different attitudes to the passing of time.			
I can explore changes in relationships described in at least two poems.			
I can discuss the ways in which some poems suggest that human nature and/or society does not change.			
I can identify which poems are sonnets and discuss their features.			
I can discuss the ways in which a strong atmosphere or sense of place are created in some poems.			
I can explore the ways in which some poets suggest that true love does not change with time.			
I can explore the ways other worlds and/or the supernatural are suggested in some poems.			

Re-read the poems that need more work, with your notes, highlighting what you don't understand. Discuss them with a partner or ask your teacher for help.

Memory joggers

This quiz will help you to:
- ✔ test your memory of the texts and their content
- ✔ identify which poems you may still need to work on
- ✔ think quickly and recall key details.

1 In which poem does a statue make the poet reflect on the past?

2 In which poem does a stolen apple feature and what happens?

3 In which poem is the past described as 'the land of lost content'?

4 Who does death lay his 'icy hand' on in **Death the Leveller**?

5 Who tells us to honour our parents because we will profit from it?

6 In which poem is a husband convinced that his wife's spirit stays with him?

7 Who is warned to get married before they lose their looks?

8 In which poem are the innocent joys of childhood like being close to heaven?

9 Who grieves over leaves falling? What does the poet really think is the problem?

10 What bird represents hope to a depressed man? Why isn't he cheered by it?

11 In which poem are people criticised for wearing fashionable clothes?

When you have finished, check your answers with your teacher or against the poems and make a note of which poems you think you need to work on more.

Thinking and linking

Exam questions will ask you to write about common themes or ideas in the poems. This activity will help you to think about the ways in which poems can be linked or grouped together.

1 Copy and complete the chart below to show which poems, in your opinion, contain the listed themes or ideas. The first one has been done for you.

2 Add other themes, e.g. 'Death' and 'Growing older', and complete these rows too.

> **! Remember**
>
> A poem may be read as having more than one theme or idea.

Theme	Poems			
Mystery	The Gray Folk	The Listeners	Woak Hill	Ozymandias
Nostalgia for the past				
Human nature and/or society				
Changing relationships				
Negative view of time and change	Ozymandias		The Darkling Thrush	

3 For each poem you have chosen, select at least three quotations that help convey the theme or idea.

4 For each quotation, add notes explaining how it helps to convey the theme or idea. For example:

> **@ Extension**
>
> Create two grids – one to show poems which treat themes in a similar way and one to show those which treat themes in a contrasting way.

Poem: 'The Gray Folk'

Quotation: suggesting mystery – 'Past lock and chain and bolt and bar'.

Explanation: this line suggests ghosts – the 'gray folk' seem to able to pass through solid objects. The fact that she has so many bolts and locks suggests she is scared of them and is trying to keep them out, but it does not work. We wonder what they are and why she is afraid.

Linking and contrasting poems

This activity will help you to:

✔ explore links and contrasts between the poems
✔ consider the range of poems you might choose from to answer a specific exam question
✔ develop your confidence that you can answer a range of exam questions.

1 Referring to your 'thinking and linking' chart, identify poems which you think could be described by each statement below.

a These two poems offer a negative view of time and change.
b These two poems express regret or nostalgia for the past.
c These two poems differ in the view of childhood they present.
d These two poems show how everything fades or changes with time.
e These two poems create a ghostly atmosphere.
f These two poems show how relationships can change for the worse.
g These two poems offer a cynical view of human nature.

2 Make detailed notes in your notebook, giving reasons for your choice of each poem. The first example has been done for you below, but you could add quotations to take this further.

3 Then compare your choices with a partner. See if you chose the same poems and compare your reasons.

These two poems offer a negative view of time and change.

Poem 1: 'The Darkling Thrush'

<u>Reasons</u>:

- uses language and images of sadness and death
- sees winter as death – seems to have forgotten spring
- the thrush is old and frail – makes me think the man must be too, as he seems to see death everywhere
- maybe the thrush is singing because it knows spring will come, but it might not for the speaker.

Poem 2: 'Ozymandias'

<u>Reasons</u>:

- shows how the most powerful forces crumble into nothing – image of a wasteland
- shows that even when we try to leave permanent reminders they end up as ruins
- message on statue is arrogant – this makes the poem ironic
- but there is hope in the way that the artist's skill is still visible – suggests it is art rather than armies which survives.

Generations

Confidence checklist

In a chart like the one below, place a tick in the appropriate column for each statement depending on how confident you feel.

Statement	Not confident	Could do more work	Very confident
I can compare poems that show relationships between parents and children.			
I can explore different attitudes to childhood in the poems.			
I can compare the ways in which poets represent the relationship between our childhood and adult selves.			
I can explore different aspects of family life in the poems.			
I can discuss the ways in which relationships between the generations are presented.			
I can explore the ways in which the feelings babies inspire are presented.			

Re-read the poems that need more work, with your notes, highlighting what you don't understand. Discuss them with a partner or ask your teacher for help.

Memory joggers

This quiz will help you to:
- ✔ test your memory of the texts and their content
- ✔ identify which poems you may still need to work on
- ✔ think quickly and recall key details.

1. Who likens his son to a stranded beetle?

2. Who describes their baby as a clown, a fish, a prawn and a bean?

3. Which poet grew up in Coventry? How does he feel about his childhood there?

4. How have the roles reversed in **Follower**?

5. Which character was cruelly treated at school? How did this affect him later?

6. Which poem presents child-like vulnerability as a disadvantage in adults?

7. Who is afraid of the baby they are caring for? Why?

8. Which poem describes the devastating effect of seeing a film of a child? Why is it devastating?

9 In which poem is the father usually caring but occasionally violent or deceitful?

10 In which poem does a man pretend his wife is still alive?

11 In which poem is the move from country to town life described and what are the similarities and differences?

When you have finished, check your answers with your teacher or against the poems and make a note of which poems you think you need to work on more.

> **! Remember**
>
> A poem may be read as having more than one theme or idea.

Thinking and linking

Exam questions will ask you to write about common themes or ideas in the poems. This activity will help you to think about the ways in which poems can be linked or grouped together.

1 Copy and complete the chart below to show which poems, in your opinion, contain the listed themes or ideas. The first one has been done for you.

2 Add other themes, e.g. 'Family life' and 'Childhood memories', and complete these rows too.

Theme	Poems			
Thoughts about babies	Clocks	You're	Baby-sitting	To Edwin, at Eight Months
Parents and children				
Death of close relatives				
The adult the child becomes				
Care for older relatives				
Special moments with children				

3 For each poem you have chosen, select at least three quotations that help convey the theme or idea.

4 For each quotation, add notes explaining how it helps to convey the theme or idea. For example:

> **@ Extension**
>
> Create two grids – one to show poems which treat themes in a similar way and one to show those which treat themes in a contrasting way.

Poem: 'Clocks'

Quotation: showing thoughts about babies – 'He blows me a field of gold/from the palm of his hand'.

Explanation: this quotation suggests that she sees this time with her baby as a golden time. The small things the baby does give her great joy. It is also like blowing a kiss, suggesting the love between them.

Annotating texts

This activity will help you to:
- ✔ revise the texts closely
- ✔ annotate usefully for the exam
- ✔ create visual revision aids.

There are some good ground rules for making useful annotation, which apply whether or not you are allowed to take annotated copies into the exam.

- Annotations can be helpful for speed and efficiency. They don't replace your knowledge, understanding and thinking – they simply help you find the examples you need when you need them.
- Don't write lots of notes. You risk regurgitating them in the exam and they make the page look jumbled. The rule of thumb is, the more you write, the less you might think.
- Choose a colour code for identifying different features and use the same code for all your annotations.

In the example below, the text has been picked out in different styles because we don't have colour. Try to decide why these parts of the text have been picked out. Add your ideas around the poem in note form. Three examples have been given to start you off.

Poem

by Simon Armitage

And if it snowed and snow covered the drive
He took a spade and it *tossed* to one side
And **always** tucked his up daughter at night
And *slippered* her the one time she lied

| Strength. |

And **every week** he tipped up half his wage
And what he didn't spend **each week** he'd save
And praised his wife for **every meal** she made
And **once**, for laughing, *punched* her in the face

| Sonnet = traditional form. |

And for his mum he hired a private nurse
And **every** Sunday taxied her to church
And he blubbed when she went from bad to worse
And **twice** he *lifted* ten quid from her purse

Here's how they rated him when they looked back:
Sometimes he did this, sometimes he did that

| Structure = two sides. |

 Extension

Ask your teacher for some clean copies of the poems in this Section. In groups or pairs, choose a poem each. Use your colour code to highlight words, phrases, images and effects that you think are interesting or important. Swap poems and create notes to explain the choice of highlights. Compare and discuss results afterwards.

The 1914–1918 War (i)

OPENING LINES

Confidence checklist

In a chart like the one below, place a tick in the appropriate column for each statement depending on how confident you feel.

Statement	Not confident	Could do more work	Very confident
I can compare two poems that show the reality of life in the trenches.			
I can explore the ways in which war affected women in at least two poems.			
I can explore soldiers' attitudes to those left at home.			
I can compare the ways in which the soldier's expectations were different from the reality of war.			
I can identify which poems are sonnets and discuss their features.			
I can discuss the ways in which life after the war is presented.			
I can explore the ways in which war affected individuals.			

Re-read the poems that need more work, with your notes, highlighting what you don't understand. Discuss them with a partner or ask your teacher for help.

Memory joggers

This quiz will help you to:
✔ test your memory of the texts and their content
✔ identify which poems you may still need to work on
✔ think quickly and recall key details.

1 In which poem does a wheelchair-bound man remember the past?

2 Of what does a young soldier sleeping remind Siegfried Sassoon?

3 Name three traditionally male jobs that women are doing in **War Girls**?

4 In which poem do soldiers look like ghosts in a film?

5 Who shows the effect of the horrors of trench warfare on minds as well as bodies?

6 What does Eleanor Farjeon send to her loved one in France? How does she hide it?

7 In which poem is the endless waiting suggested: 'But nothing happens'?

8 Who was shot when he raised his head to take a bet? What was the bet?

9 In which poem is the rain 'full of ghosts … that tap and sign/Upon the glass'?

10 Which poem shows the effect of the war on country life?

11 Which poem describes dreams of heroism as 'babes at play'?

12 Who accuses majors of being greedy hypocrites who die safely in bed?

When you have finished, check your answers with your teacher or against the poems and make a note of which poems you think you need to work on more.

Thinking and linking

Exam questions will ask you to write about common themes or ideas in the poems. This activity will help you think about ways in which poems can be linked or grouped.

Remember

A poem may be read as having more than one theme or idea.

1 Copy and complete the chart below to show which poems, in your opinion, contain the listed themes or ideas. The first one has been done for you.

2 Add other themes, e.g. 'Patriotism' and complete these rows too.

Theme	Poems			
The reality of the trenches	Mental cases	The Dug-Out	Exposure	Breakfast
Anger at those who promote war	Base details			
Women and the war				
What war does to the individual	Easter Monday			
The effects of war on nature	Sonnet	Mental Cases		
The after-effects of war				

Extension

Create two grids – one to show poems which treat themes in a similar way and one to show those which treat themes in a contrasting way.

3 For each poem you have chosen, select at least three quotations that help convey the theme or idea.

4 For each quotation, add notes explaining how it helps to convey the theme or idea. For example:

Poem: 'Mental Cases'

Quotation: Showing reality of trenches – 'Treading blood from lungs that had loved laughter'.

Explanation: this paints a picture of how the men had to walk across corpses. 'Treading blood' is very graphic and conveys the horror of the experience. The fact that the dead had 'loved laughter' shows the soldiers thought about how the bodies were once people who loved life.

Linking and contrasting poems

This activity will help you to:

✔ revise contrasts and links between the poems

✔ structure your thinking about the poems

✔ focus on techniques used to express ideas in essays.

1 Make a chart like the example below.

2 Choose a theme from your 'thinking and linking' chart and two poems which offer contrasting views/ideas on that theme. The poems do not have to actually disagree, they can offer a different perspective on a subject.

3 For each poem:

a summarise the views or ideas in each poem.

b consider the ways in which these are conveyed to the reader – you must include at least two different techniques and offer supporting quotations.

c explain your own response to each view.

Theme: the after effects of war Mental Cases	Sonnet
Gives a shocking picture of the long-term effects of the horrors of war on men's minds.	Shows the effect of war on one woman: the sadness she will live with for the rest of her life.
Ways the view or idea is conveyed	
1 Starts by asking a question, 'Who are these?' and answers in the next two stanzas with who they are and why they are like that. (structure)	1 Creates a sense of intimacy at the start by describing 'lips' and 'arms'. We get the idea of her thinking of the lovers of her youth. (language)
2 Uses dramatic and horrific imagery to convey how the experience had driven the soldiers insane, e.g. 'wading sloughs of flesh' and 'carnage incomparable'. (imagery)	2 Uses the metaphor of the lonely tree that doesn't remember which birds have vanished, but stands alone and misses them. (imagery)
3 Uses alliteration to create a sense of what the men can still see and hear, e.g. 'Memory fingers in their hair of murders' and 'blood from lungs that had loved laughter'. (alliteration)	3 The final line links youth with summer: the alliteration of 'summer sang ... sings no more' creates a sad and musical sound. (language/alliteration)
My response to each view	
Horror at the graphic descriptions of death; I can see the guilt of those who sent them there or who participated in the last line; by calling the reader 'brother', Owen implies we are all guilty for taking part or for allowing war to happen.	This poem reminds me of all the women who lost the loves of their youth and faced the rest of their lives alone. A part of her life – the beautiful summer part – died with all the young men.

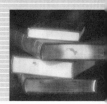

Men and Women
• English Lit: Unit 6
• 45 mins to answer
• Choice of 3 questions
• Worth 25% of mark

Tackling the question

Choose *two* poems from the list below which offer views on the ending of relationships. Explore the thoughts and feelings about the ending of relationships expressed by the two poets and the ways in which they communicate these.

- • **Faithless Sally Brown**
- • **Remember**
- • **They flee from me ...'**
- • **In the Mile End Road**

 2 MINS

1 Choosing your question

When choosing your exam question, there are two things to ask yourself:
- • do I understand what the question is asking me to do
- • do I know enough about the texts to be able to answer the question well?

To answer this exam question, you will need to:
- ✔ be familiar with the idea of the ending of relationships in the poetry
- ✔ be able to identify this theme in at least two of the poems on the list
- ✔ feel confident that you can write about the ways the poets suggest their ideas and feelings about the end of love.

Do you feel confident you can answer the question successfully? If not, look at the other questions to see if you feel more confident with them.

2 MINS

2 Choosing the poems

You should know all the poems in the list equally well. To choose the best poems to answer the question, ask yourself:
- • which offer similar views and/or feelings
- • which have contrasting views and/or feelings
- • which use similar or contrasting language and/or techniques?

This will help you focus on the key aspects of successful writing about poetry right from the start and will help you plan your points.

So, you might write about **In the Mile End Road** and **Remember** because:
- ✔ they both show feelings about the ending of a relationship through death
- ✔ they offer contrasting feelings/views
- ✔ they use different techniques to do this.

Or, you might write about **They flee from me ...** and **Faithless Sally Brown** because:
- ✔ they both offer views on women as fickle, flitting from one relationship to another
- ✔ one is a ballad telling a story to make its point and one is a formally structured poem offering a personal view.

! Remember

Planning helps you think up and sort out your ideas and improves the structure and focus of your essays.

⏱ 3 Planning your answer

You will need to make a quick outline plan to help you structure your ideas. The poems '**They flee from me ...**' and '**Faithless Sally Brown**' are used below to explore the techniques.

a Underline the key words in the question.

> Choose *two* poems which offer views on the <u>ending of relationships</u>. Explore the thoughts and feelings about the ending of relationships <u>expressed by</u> the two poets, and <u>the ways</u> in which they communicate these.

Key ideas to concentrate on

Focus of my points

Decide what the key words mean and think about what you are being asked to comment on. For example:

- the ending of relationships – what the poems are about
- language – the words and phrases, how images are created
- technique – other interesting aspects of the poem such as form, imagery and pace.

b Brainstorm ideas and make a few notes for each of your poems. Jot down some reminders about textual details and quotations you could use to support these points.

If you prefer to plan using bullets points, look at the examples of using this technique on pages 33 and 38.

◎ Extension

Create brainstorms for the other pairs of poems suggested for this question.

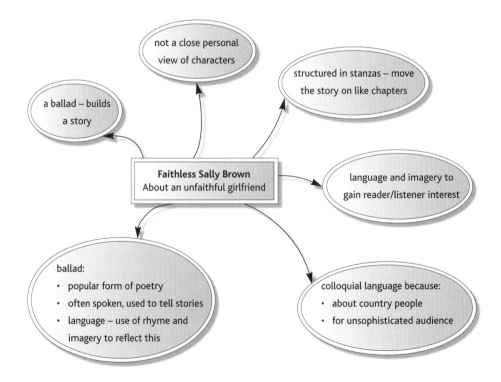

not a close personal view of characters

a ballad – builds a story

structured in stanzas – move the story on like chapters

Faithless Sally Brown
About an unfaithful girlfriend

language and imagery to gain reader/listener interest

ballad:
- popular form of poetry
- often spoken, used to tell stories
- language – use of rhyme and imagery to reflect this

colloquial language because:
- about country people
- for unsophisticated audience

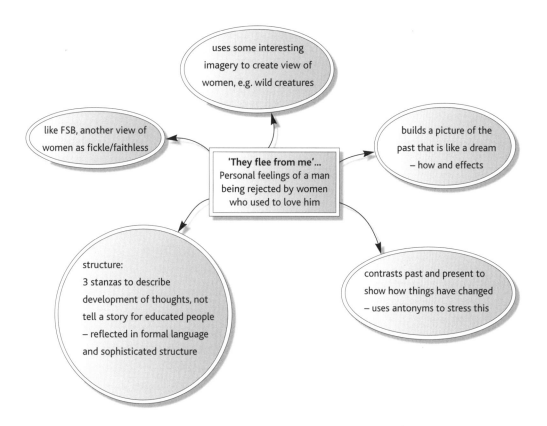

uses some interesting imagery to create view of women, e.g. wild creatures

like FSB, another view of women as fickle/faithless

'They flee from me'... Personal feelings of a man being rejected by women who used to love him

builds a picture of the past that is like a dream – how and effects

structure:
3 stanzas to describe development of thoughts, not tell a story for educated people – reflected in formal language and sophisticated structure

contrasts past and present to show how things have changed – uses antonyms to stress this

---

Top tip

Use your plan to keep your answer on track.

c Working from the brainstorms, decide how you would order the points. Would you write about one poem, followed by the other, or focus for example on attitude, form and then language in paragraphs on both poems? What would be the benefits and drawbacks of each approach?

Give each point on the brainstorms a number according to the order in which you would write about them. Discuss and compare your ideas with a partner.

! Remember

An introduction shows the examiner your overall approach and guides them into what you think about the poems.

30 MINS **4 Writing your answer**

a **Opening paragraph**
First, introduce both of your poems and the aspect of the ending of relationships that each deals with. Don't state the obvious, for example: 'I am going to write about ...'. Start your answer with a crisper first sentence and then give a brief overview in one or two more sentences. For example:

Top tip

Keep introductions brief and clear, leave the detail to your main answer.

'They flee from me ...' and 'Faithless Sally Brown' both offer a view of relationships ending because of the fickle behaviour of women. 'Faithless Sally Brown' is a ballad telling of a woman who finds a new love when her boyfriend is press-ganged into the navy, whereas 'They Flee from me ...' is a sonnet about a man's feelings when he is rejected by women who once loved him.

b   Following paragraphs
- ✔ Keep the question in view and in mind throughout.
- ✔ Follow your plan of the points you are going to make and the order in which you are going to deal with them.
- ✔ Start each new paragraph with a point which clearly relates to the question.

Use the three-point formula, for example:

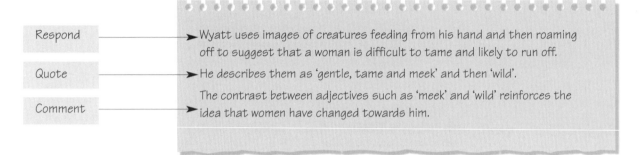

Respond	Wyatt uses images of creatures feeding from his hand and then roaming off to suggest that a woman is difficult to tame and likely to run off.
Quote	He describes them as 'gentle, tame and meek' and then 'wild'.
Comment	The contrast between adjectives such as 'meek' and 'wild' reinforces the idea that women have changed towards him.

 Remember

It's ok if your ideas about the feelings in the poems are different from those here. The examiner is genuinely interested in what you think, not expecting one 'right' answer.

Top tips

- Check that your 'comments' are the longest parts of your paragraphs. If they aren't, spend more time developing your ideas.
- Make sure your 'comment' is focused on details such as the language which shows how the poet is suggesting ideas, and is not just a repeat of your 'respond' point. Try focusing on one or two words from your quotation and broaden out your comments from there.
- It's better to say a lot about a little, not the other way round. You cannot say everything that could be said about the poems, so aim to write about two or three things in detail.

c   Final paragraph
- ✔ Refer to both poems.
- ✔ Try to offer a fresh perspective so you are not just summing up and repeating yourself, for example:

    Both poems are more complex than they first appear: the speaker in 'They flee from me ...' is presented as a hunter as well as a victim; in 'Faithless Sally Brown', Ben is mocked as well as Sally.

- ✔ Try to offer a personal response. You could explain:
    - which poem you found most effective and why
    - which aspects of the poems you feel are the most interesting
    - which poem is closest to your own views or feelings
    - how a poem offers you new ideas or views of something you might not have thought about before.

5 Checking your answer

Errors cost marks so it is worth taking the time to check your written expression and the spelling of all names. Correct any other slips of the pen and add any after thoughts showing clearly where they go.

Looking at candidates' answers

1 Using your own experience, and the guidance offered so far, what advice would you give to each of these students, based on the following extracts from their answers?

2 Take the points made by either of these candidates and explore them more fully following the three-point formula.

Zein

In They flee from me I think the poet is trying to show that women don't think he is attractive any more because they run away like wild animals. All he has got is his memories like when she kissed him and took off her night-gown. This is a very sensual image. He shows that women just want change 'now they range busily seeking with a continual change' and 'newfangledness'. He suggests they don't think he is attractive any more because he is too gentle with them 'but all is turned through my gentleness' and says at the end that they deserve worse than him. This is like modern men saying 'treat 'em mean keep 'em keen.

Hannah

I think both the poems are trying to make points. They flee from me shows us a man who is feeling angry and sorry for himself. He suggests the reason women leave him is because he treats them kindly, but they are more like animals than rational creatures, and are only satisfied with change and variety. There are times though, when he is not such a victim as he appears – he describes them as putting 'themselves in danger' by coming to him, which suggests he is a predator. This contrasts with the description of women 'stalking in my chamber'. The word 'stalking' presents women as the hunters and 'my chamber' suggests it is the man who is hunted. I think this poem is about a man who is looking for the reasons his relationships end, and he finds someone else to blame. He defends himself by describing his 'gentleness', and states twice that women are always looking for change. The final two lines show his bitterness.

Examiner's comments

<u>Zein's</u> work shows he understands the poem. He makes a range of points and refers to details to support them, sometimes quoting. However, he needs to separate out his ideas and follow the three-point formula to allow himself to explore his ideas fully. His phrase at the end is too colloquial for an exam.
Working towards Grade D.

<u>Hannah's</u> work is more assured in style, but still needs to separate, support and explore some of her points. The opening comment leads nowhere and she summarises, rather than examines, the ideas which follow. The comments on 'stalking in my chamber' are much better dealt with – she needs to adopt this approach with her other points.
Working towards Grade B.

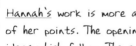

Higher Tier, Question 2
OPENING LINES

Tackling the question

> With careful reference to the language used in each poem, explore what **War Girls** and **In Time of War** suggest about women's reactions to war and about their roles in it.

2 MINS 1 Choosing your question

When choosing your exam question, there are two things to ask yourself:
- do I understand what the question is asking me to do
- do I know enough about the texts to be able to answer the question well?

To answer this exam question, you will need to:
- ✔ be familiar with the themes of women's reactions and/or roles in war in the poems listed
- ✔ feel confident that you can write about the ways the poets use language to suggest and/or explore women's reactions to war and roles in it.

Do you feel confident you can answer the question successfully? If not, look at the other questions to see if you feel more confident with them.

> **! Remember**
>
> You will lose marks if you do not answer the question fully or if you give a partial response because you can't apply the question to the texts.

10 MINS 2 Planning your answer

You will need to make a quick outline plan to help you structure your ideas.

a   Underline the key words in the question.

Explore in my points

Key ideas to concentrate on

> With careful reference to the <u>language used</u> in each poem, explore what **War Girls** and **In Time of War** suggest about <u>women's reactions to war</u> and about <u>their roles in it</u>.

Decide what the key words mean and think about what you are being asked to comment on. For example:
- women's attitudes to war – pro, anti, fearful, patriotic?
- women's roles in war – expectations of women, showing your knowledge of social/historical background and how reflected in the poems
- language – how the poets' words, phrases and images work to suggest meaning to the reader.

b   List your ideas on each poem as bullet points (perhaps shorter notes than those on the next page). Jot down some reminders about textual details and quotations you could use to support these points.

If you prefer to plan using brainstorming, look at the examples of using this technique on pages 28, 61, 71 and 75.

Extension

Create lists for the other poems suggested by this theme.

War Girls

- about women taking on traditionally male jobs during the war
- cheerful and patriotic in tone
- lots of active verbs – women active, not sentimental and passive
- adjectives describe a new view of young women – not traditional female qualities
- new freedom for women – liberation from traditional roles
- jobs, working class
- a propaganda poem? – to get young working class women to take on this work, to keep their spirits up?
- traditional female qualities underneath suggested
- things will change back when the men return?

 Remember

Planning helps you think up and sort out your ideas and improves the structure and focus of your essays.

In Time of War

- personal feelings of a woman whose partner or husband is away at war
- woman as passively waiting – full of fear
- used to have an immature view of war and of love, now she knows the reality
- sense of real relationship, not girlhood dream of a hero
- strong imagery of fear, 'blind'
- 'render' – she has to give him up for war; it's not like she thought it would be – 'do gloriously for my sake'
- all she can do is pray – repetition shows desperation
- slow and thoughtful pace
- first stanza flows smoothly, second more broken – reinforces contrasts between fantasy and reality.

Top tip

Use your plan to keep your answer on track.

c Working from your bullet lists, decide how you would order the points. Would you write about one poem, followed by the other, or focus for example on attitude, form and then language in paragraphs on both poems? What would be the benefits and drawbacks of each approach?

Give each point on the bullet lists a number according to the order in which you would write about them. Discuss and compare your ideas with a partner.

3 Writing your answer

! Remember

An introduction shows the examiner your overall approach and guides them into what you think about the poems.

a   Opening paragraph

First, introduce both of your poems and the aspect of the ending of relationships that each deals with. Don't state the obvious, for example: 'I am going to write about …'. Start your answer with a crisper first sentence and then give a brief overview in one or two more sentences. For example:

> 'War Girls' and 'In Time of War' offer contrasting pictures both of women's roles in war and their reactions to it. 'War Girls' is cheerful and patriotic, and presents women as having a vital and active role in the war, whereas 'In Time of War' presents women as fearful and passive, only able to pray for men's return.

☀ Top tip

Keep introductions brief and clear; leave the detail to the main part of your answer.

Looking at candidates' opening paragraphs

Read through the examples below and answer the following questions:
*   which is closest to the guidelines above
*   what mistakes do the other two make
*   what advice would you give to them?

> Karis
>
> The two poems, 'War Girls', and 'In Time of War' both display very different reactions to the war. The first tends to focus upon the roles that women have been left to fill whilst the men are fighting in the Great War, whilst the second focuses on the emotions caused by her partner risking his life to fight for his country and the longing and admiration she feels for him.

> Ashley
>
> 'War Girls' is about women working – 'They're going to keep their end up' – whereas the second poem, 'In Time of War' is more concerned with emotion, with a focus on a woman wanting her partner to return – 'God bring you back'.

> Owen
>
> If we look at the first poem we see the suffragette-like attitude towards work, the acceptance of a need for women to do their duty and take on the role of men as protectors of the economy, bringing with it responsibility and greater personal freedom.

b   Following paragraphs
*   ✔ Keep the question in view and in mind throughout.
*   ✔ Follow your plan of the points you are going to make and the order in which you are going to deal with them.

✔ Start each new paragraph with a point which clearly relates to the question. Use the writers' names and focus on the techniques they use rather than just telling the story.

✔ Use the three-point formula, for example:

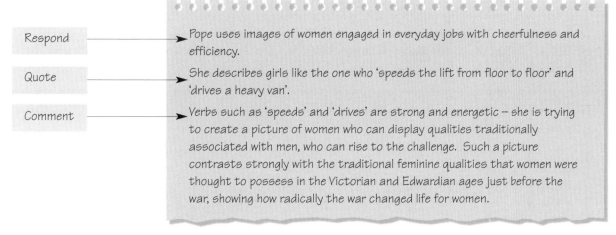

Respond → Pope uses images of women engaged in everyday jobs with cheerfulness and efficiency.

Quote → She describes girls like the one who 'speeds the lift from floor to floor' and 'drives a heavy van'.

Comment → Verbs such as 'speeds' and 'drives' are strong and energetic – she is trying to create a picture of women who can display qualities traditionally associated with men, who can rise to the challenge. Such a picture contrasts strongly with the traditional feminine qualities that women were thought to possess in the Victorian and Edwardian ages just before the war, showing how radically the war changed life for women.

! Remember

It's ok if your ideas about the feelings in the poems are different from those here. The examiner is genuinely interested in what you think, not expecting one 'right' answer.

💡 Top tips

- Check that your 'comments' are the longest parts of your paragraphs. If they aren't, spend more time developing your ideas.
- Make sure your 'comment' is focused on details such as the language which shows how the poet is suggesting ideas, and is not just a repeat of your 'respond' point. Try focusing on one or two words from your quotation and broaden out your comments from there.
- It's better to say a lot about a little, not the other way round. You cannot say everything that could be said about the poems, so aim to write about two or three things in detail.

c **Final paragraph**

Follow the guidelines on page 45. Try to offer a fresh perspective, for example:

'Perhaps 'In Time of War' is the more honest of the two poems – it shows the real fear many women must have had, whereas 'War Girls' seems to assume that the boys will 'come marching back'.

 ## 4 Checking your answer

Errors cost marks so take the time to check the aspects listed on page 45.

Looking at candidates' answers

Using your own experience, and the guidance offered so far, what advice would you give to Karis and Deanne, based on the extracts from their answers on page 36?

Karis

'War Girls' has a theme of women's unity and a sense of collaboration in crisis, 'They're going to keep their end up'. The poem suggests these women were full of motivation. 'They're out to show their grit'. This does also suggest though that besides diverting crisis by working for the men that are fighting for the country, they are just as much making the most of the opportunity to show their abilities in such a situation, which up to this point they had not been able to do. Now they have 'no time for love and kisses'.

Contrast this with 'In Time of War' where the woman is thinking only about her own position and how much she misses her partner 'so knit with all I am or do' implying that her partner is a part of herself. This is a much more self-centred poem.

Deanne

In Jessie Pope's poem the language is simple and colloquial. This suggests an everyday tone, and supports the idea of working people.

'And tackle jobs with energy and knack'

The girls in the poem are shown not only to be taking on the jobs of men, but doing it cheerfully and well. 'energy' and 'knack' especially suggest this. This is contrasted by the woman in 'In Time of War', for whom wartime is unbearably emotional.

'But now I render, blind with fear'

'Render' suggests she gives him up because she has no choice, and 'blind' is very emotive, showing how scared women were to do this. Enjoyment of everyday life is not even considered.

Examiner's comments

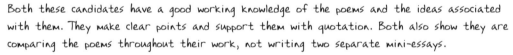

Both these candidates have a good working knowledge of the poems and the ideas associated with them. They make clear points and support them with quotation. Both also show they are comparing the poems throughout their work, not writing two separate mini-essays.

Karis starts with a well made point, but she needs to introduce the quotation properly in a sentence, not just plonk it in, in a phrase like 'Pope describes how ...'. The key mistake she makes here is not to follow up the quotation with comment or explanation. How does this example show unity or collaboration? Is it in the use of 'they' or 'their'? She does follow her next point and quotation with a comment, but the three are not very well linked. Does the quotation really suggest all she says, and if so, how? She establishes a good area of contrast with the other poem, but again fails to follow up with close exploration of language. This is especially important because the question specifically asks for it.

Working towards Grade C.

Deanne also offers an interesting area of contrast. She follows the three-point formula efficiently, though her first quotation, like Karis', needs to be properly embedded in her work. The last sentence of her paragraph is the weakest part - she would do better to focus on what this poem is about, rather than just saying what isn't there. This is an easy trap to fall into when contrasting poems.

Working towards Grade C.

Time and Change
- English/English Lit: Unit 6
- 45 mins to answer
- Choice of 3 questions
- Worth 25% of mark

Tackling the question

> What feelings about the past do any *two* poems from the list below suggest to you? How do the words of each poet make these feelings clear to you?
> - I Remember, I Remember
> - Ozymandias
> - 'Into my heart ...'
> - The Gray Folk

1 Choosing your question

When choosing your exam question, there are two things to ask yourself:
- do I understand what the question is asking me to do
- do I know enough about the texts to be able to answer the question well?

To answer this exam question, you will need to:
- ✔ be familiar with the idea of attitudes to the past
- ✔ be able to identify this theme in at least two of the poems on the list
- ✔ feel confident that you can write about the ways the poets suggest their ideas and feelings about the past.

Do you feel confident you can answer the question successfully? If not, look at the other questions to see if you feel more confident with them.

! Remember

You will lose marks if you do not answer the question fully or if you give a partial response because you can't apply the question to the texts.

2 Choosing the poems

You should know all the poems in the list equally well. To choose the best poems to answer the question, ask yourself:
- which have similar ideas and feelings
- which use similar images
- which have different attitudes
- which use different ways of showing the different attitudes?

This will help you focus on the key aspects of successful writing about poetry right from the start and will help you plan your points.

Try pairing the poems on the list in different combinations to answer the question, as in the examples below. Note down a couple of bullet points to show what aspects might be interesting to write about.

So, you might write about **I Remember, I Remember** and **'Into My heart ...'** because:
- ✔ they are both about being happier in the past
- ✔ they both use images linked with the countryside/nature
- ✔ they use interesting metaphors.

Or, you might write about **Ozymandias** and **The Gray Folk** because:
- ✔ they both create a sense of mystery about the past
- ✔ they both use landscape.

Extension

Try the pairing activity for different questions and with a suitable list of possible poems.

Or, you might write about **I Remember, I Remember** and **Ozymandias** because:

✔ one gives a very personal, emotional view and one is about rulers and empires
✔ they both have a message about what could be really important in life.

3 Planning your answer

You need to make a quick outline plan to help you structure your ideas. The poems **Ozymandias** and '**Into my heart ...**' are used below to explore the techniques.

a Underline the key words in the question.

Key word to concentrate on

Focus of the points I make

> What feelings about the past do any *two* poems from the list below suggest to you? How do the words of each poet make these feelings clear to you?

Decide what the key words mean and think about what you are being asked to comment on. For example:

- attitudes to the past: what views of the past we are given and how do the poets seem to feel about the past?
- how do the poets suggest their ideas to the reader; what language, images and techniques do they use?

Remember

Planning helps you think up and sort out your ideas and improves the structure and focus of your essays.

Top tips

- Use your plan to keep your answer on track.
- Foundation Tier questions often have a 'what' part on the ideas and feelings in the poems, and a 'how' part on the language and structure. Don't write about the two separately, but if you focus more closely on the words and shape of the poems, you will be highly rewarded.

b List your ideas on each poem as bullet points (perhaps shorter notes than those below). Jot down some reminders about textual details and quotations you could use to support these points.

Ozymandias

- about a ruined statue in the desert
- attitude – that nothing lasts forever, no matter how powerful and great
- Ozymandias thought he was very powerful: 'sneer', 'cold command'
- language used to emphasise ruin
- sets up a mystery: mysterious traveller, statue just legs – who is he?; no great city, just a desert – what happened to the city?
- Lack of punctuation – flows like thoughts; or could be the breathless traveller's excitement: pause before final line – serious effect
- uses irony: the inscription was to tell everyone who read it how powerful he was, but it tells the poet and the reader how power is temporary

- sands are like time – they cover everything eventually
- suggests artists, not kings, might be the ones whose work lives longest (we can still see the sculptor's skill); could this mean poets write to leave something lasting?

Extension

Try creating a sample essay plan by copying and cutting up the points, and experimenting with different orders.

Into my heart

- about regret for the past
- the past described as a landscape – an extended metaphor
- language and images make landscape seem ideal, rural
- like a fairy tale 'land of lost content'
- some poetic language – about a strong feeling, not a realistic description of a single strong memory
- two stanzas – one asks a question, the next answers it
- painful to think of the past – like difficulty breathing
- final line gives the reason for the pain – nostalgia.

Extension

Create planning notes for the other pairs of poems suggested for this question.

If you prefer to plan using brainstorming, look at the examples of using this technique on pages 33 and 38.

c   Working from the bullet lists, decide how you would order the points. Would you write about one poem, followed by the other, or focus for example on attitude, form and then language in paragraphs on both poems? What would be the benefits and drawbacks of each approach?

Give each point on the bullet lists a number according to the order in which you would write about them. Discuss and compare your ideas with a partner.

🕰️ 4 Writing your answer

a   **Opening paragraph**
First, introduce both of your poems and briefly describe the attitude to the past in each. Don't state the obvious, for example: 'I am going to write about ...'. Start your answer with a crisper first sentence and then give a brief overview in one or two more sentences. For example:

Remember

An introduction shows the examiner your overall approach and guides them into what you think about the poems.

'Ozymandias' and 'Into my heart' are interesting to compare because they show different attitudes to the past. 'Ozymandias' uses the image of a ruined statue and a lost kingdom to suggest that nobody lasts forever no matter how powerful they are. 'Into my heart' is much more personal, and shows us how we can long for the happiness of the past which we can never experience again.

b **Following paragraphs**
- ✔ Keep the question in view and in mind throughout.
- ✔ Follow your plan of the points you are going to make and the order in which you are going to deal with them.
- ✔ Start each new paragraph with a point which clearly relates to the question.
- ✔ Use the writers' names and focus on the techniques they use rather than just telling the story.
- ✔ Use the three-point formula, for example:

Respond

Quote

Comment

> Shelley shows us that even the most powerful cannot beat time.
>
> He gives us an idea of Ozymandias' power through descriptions such as 'sneer of cold command'.
>
> The word 'sneer' suggests Ozymandias was arrogant and 'cold command' shows he was used to getting his own way, and was unfeeling. This helps to make the point that even a great ruler ends up crumbled into nothing. The inscription on the statue continues this idea ...

Top tips

- Check that your 'comments' are the longest parts of your paragraphs. If they aren't, spend more time developing your ideas.
- Make sure your 'comment' is focused on details such as the language which shows how the poet is suggesting ideas, and is not just a repeat of your 'respond' point. Try focusing on one or two words from your quotation and broaden out your comments from there.
- It's better to say a lot about a little, not the other way round. You cannot say everything that could be said about the poems, so aim to write about two or three things in detail.

c **Final paragraph**
Follow the guidelines on page 45. Try to offer a personal response, for example:

> I found the idea in 'Ozymandias' that even the most powerful people and empires crumble into nothing appealed to me. It made me think about powerful countries in modern times. Perhaps I liked this poem best because it is harder for me to relate to the idea of nostalgia, although one day I will look on my school days as a happy land that I can never go back to.

5 Checking your answer

Errors cost marks so it is worth the time to check:

✔ written expression.

✔ spelling of the names of the authors and the characters.

✔ other slips of the pen such as punctuation problems or words missed out.

✔ add any afterthoughts that occur to you as you read through to the end of the answer and indicate clearly, using an asterisk, numbers or letters, where they should be included.

Looking at candidates' answers

Using your own experience, and the guidance offered so far, what advice would you give to each of these students, based on these extracts from their answers?

Danielle

The attitude to the past in 'Ozymandias' is that even if you are rich and powerful you will still die and there will be nothing left of you. The statue is just legs and a head and the writing on it shows he was really powerful. There is no city left just the desert 'the lone and level sands stretch far away'. Everything is gone just the statue left for tourists to look at and wonder about. In 'Into my heart' the man wants to go back to the past but he can't 'and cannot come again' because the past is like a far away land 'far yon country' This is a sad poem because he was much happier then his memories make him feel sad like 'an air that kills' blowing in his heart.

Starts well when she sums up the attitude in the poem.

Needs to follow three-point formula and introduce and explain quotation fully.

She sums up the next poem here – both the summaries would work well in an introduction.

Tells us what's in the poem instead of showing us how ideas and attitudes are suggested.

Needs to explore points more.

Needs to explore points more.

Makes a point and uses a quotation but doesn't comment on the words that do the work.

Ephraim

We can tell that this is going to be a sad poem about the past because the first line starts 'into my heart an air that kills' This is a metaphor for a painful feeling. When he writes 'yon far country' the language is old fashioned and it sounds like a fairy tale so we think he is not writing about a real place. This is another metaphor because the past is described as a far off country you can't go to. Houseman writes 'the blue remembered hills'. 'blue' could mean sad like the blues, and it is also the colour mountains look from a distance. They are not real hills it is another metaphor. 'Ozymandias' uses the landscape too to show time is like sand in the desert because it covers everything up. He describes 'lone and level sands' where a city used to be so it is a metaphor as well as a real place.

Explores this well – swapped order to Quote – Respond – Comment, but this works here.

Makes clear link to the next poem – good approach to comparison.

Starts well with three-point formula.

Explores language well here, although could lead with a stronger point than 'Houseman writes'.

Third time metaphor identified – it's good to use technical terms, but needs others too, alliteration in 'lone and level' here.

Generations
- English/English Lit: Unit 2
- 45 mins to answer
- Choice of 3 questions
- Worth 25% of mark

Tackling the question

> What feelings about the relationships between adults and children do the poets express in the two poems below? How do the words of the poets bring these feelings alive for you?

You're by Sylvia Plath

Clownlike, happiest on your hands, | Happy images.
Feet to the stars, and moon-skulled,
Gilled like a fish. A common-sense
Thumbs-down on the dodo's mode. | Her family not dying out.
5 Wrapped up in yourself like a spool, | Mystery.
Trawling your dark as owls do.
Mute as a turnip from the Fourth
Of July to All Fools' Day,
O high-riser, my little loaf.
10 Vague as fog and looked for like mail. | Expectation.
Farther off than Australia.
Bent-backed atlas, our traveled prawn.
Snug as a bud and at home | Pleased to be pregnant.
Like a sprat in a pickle jug.
15 A creel of eels, all ripples. | Imagining what baby looks like.
Jumpy as a Mexican bean.
Right, like a well-done sum. | A new life.
A clean slate, with your own face on. | A sense of baby already as an individual.

Baby-sitting by Gillian Clarke

I am sitting in a strange room listening | Starts with sense of distance.
For the wrong baby. I don't love
This baby. She is sleeping a snuffly
Roseate, bubbling sleep; she is fair; | Unfeeling language matches start.
5 She is a perfectly acceptable child. | Fear underneath coldness.
I am afraid of her. If she wakes
She will hate me. She will shout
Her hot midnight rage, her nose | Revolting image.
Will stream disgustingly and the perfume
10 Of her breath will fail to enchant me.

To her I will represent absolute
Abandonment. For her it will be worse
Than for the lover cold in lonely | Sense of touch to create image.
Sheets; worse than for the woman who waits

15 A moment to collect her dignity
Beside the bleached bone in the terminal ward.
As she rises <u>sobbing from the monstrous land</u>
Stretching for <u>milk-familiar comforting,</u>
She will find me and between us two
20 <u>It will not come. It will not come.</u>

> Strong image to show baby's despair.

> Describes a mother–baby relationship.

> Repetition to show: useless to try, frustration, giving up?

! Remember

You will lose marks if you do not answer the question fully or if you give a partial response because you can't apply the question to the texts.

1 Choosing your question

When choosing your exam question, there are two things to ask yourself:
- do I understand what the question is asking me to do
- do I know enough about the texts to be able to answer the question well?

Do you feel confident you can answer the question successfully? If not, look at the other questions to see if you feel more confident with them.

The advantages of having the poems printed on the exam paper are that:
- you have both the poems on the same page and don't have to keep checking different pages in your copy of **Opening Lines**
- you can make fresh notes on the poem that focus on the question – but don't spend too long – remember to leave time to plan and answer the question.

2 Planning your answer

You need to make a quick outline plan to help you structure your ideas.

a Underline the key words in the question.

> Key word to concentrate on

> Focus of the points I make

What feelings about the <u>relationships between adults and children</u> do the <u>poets express</u> in the two poems below? <u>How do the words</u> of the poets bring these feelings alive for you?

b Make notes on the poems. One candidate's notes have been added to the poems starting on page 42. Look at these notes and think about:
- why these parts of the poems have been picked out
- how the notes relate to the question
- what notes you might make.

c Create a plan from your notes. When you have made some notes on the poems think about:
- the overall feeling, mood or attitude in each poem
- techniques the poets have used, especially in the parts you have highlighted
- points of similarity and contrast
- how you will order your ideas.

The chart on page 44 gives you an example of the sorts of ideas you might wish to include. This will help with your revision, even though you will not have time to make a chart in the exam.

@ Extension

Create a similar chart for a different pair of poems. Try writing the ideas for this plan as a short list of bullet points or a brainstorm.

Ideas	You're	Baby-sitting
Mood or feelings in relationships	Expectation, excitement	Distance, disgust, fear
Techniques	• Simile and metaphor • Alliteration • Assonance	• Imagery • Metaphor • Alliteration
Similarities	Both about feelings for babies	
Contrasts	• Excited	• Distant
	• Her baby	• Not her baby
	• Happy images	• Images of loneliness and death
	• Fast, happy rhythm	• Slow, thoughtful rhythm
	• Talking to her baby	• Present tense – talking to herself, describing feelings and fears
	• Imagines what baby will look like	• Imagines how the baby will feel if she wakes up

d Working from the chart:
• find evidence for the points or features noted
• decide on the order in which you would use the points.

30 MINS 3 Writing your answer

a **Opening paragraph**
First, introduce both of your poems and briefly describe the attitude to the past in each. Don't state the obvious, for example: '*I am going to write about ...*'. Start your answer with a crisper first sentence and then give a brief overview in one or two more sentences. For example:

> 'You're' and 'Baby-sitting' show very different perspectives on relationships between adults and children. 'You're' is a poem written by a mother to her unborn baby and it shows her happiness, excitement and curiosity. 'Baby-sitting' shows us the feelings of a girl or woman looking after a baby which is not her own, and the relationship is distant and full of fear.

b Following paragraphs

✔ Keep the question in view and in mind throughout.

✔ Follow your plan of the points you are going to make and the order in which you are going to deal with them.

✔ Start each new paragraph with a point which clearly relates to the question.

✔ Use the writers' names and focus on the techniques they use rather than just telling the story.

✔ Use the three-point formula, for example:

Respond ───▶ Plath imagines waiting for her baby is like waiting for the post to arrive.

Quote ───▶ She describes the baby as 'looked for like mail'.

Comment ───▶ The words 'looked for' in this simile suggest expecting a letter you would really want. The idea suggests impatience and anticipation.

Top tips

• Check that your 'comments' are the longest parts of your paragraphs. If they aren't, spend more time developing your ideas.

• Make sure your 'comment' is focused on details such as the language which shows how the poet is suggesting ideas, and is not just a repeat of your 'respond' point. Try focusing on one or two words from your quotation and broaden out your comments from there.

• It's better to say a lot about a little, not the other way round. You cannot say everything that could be said about the poems, so aim to write about two or three things in detail.

c Final paragraph

• Refer to both poems.

• Try to offer a fresh perspective so you are not just summing up and repeating yourself.

• Try to offer a personal response. You could explain:

 – which poem you found most effective and why

 – which aspects of the poems you feel are the most interesting

 – which poem is closest to your own views or feelings

 – how a poem offers you new ideas or views of something you might not have thought about before.

4 Checking your answer

Errors cost marks so it is worth taking the time to check:

• written expression

• spelling of the names of the authors and the characters

• other slips of the pen such as punctuation problems or words missed out

• add any afterthoughts that occur to you as you read through to the end of the answer and indicate clearly, using an asterisk, numbers or letters, where they should be included.

Poetry for examination in
2006–2008*

War
OPENING LINES

Confidence checklist

In a chart like the one below, place a tick in the appropriate column for each statement depending on how confident you feel.

Statement	Not confident	Could do more work	Very confident
I can compare two poems that show different attitudes to war.			
I can explore the ways killing and/or death in battle is presented in at least two poems.			
I can explore the ways in which a negative view of war is expressed in some poems.			
I can discuss poems that suggest war is glorious and heroic.			
I can identify and discuss irony in some poems.			
I can discuss interesting imagery in a range of poems.			
I can explore the ways in which attitudes to war have changed or stayed the same over time.			
I can explore the ways some poets present grief and loss through war.			

Re-read the poems that need more work, with your notes, highlighting what you don't understand. Discuss them with a partner or ask your teacher for help.

Memory joggers

This quiz will help you to:
- ✔ test your memory of the texts and their content
- ✔ identify which poems you may still need to work on
- ✔ think quickly and recall key details.

1. In which poem does the poet put war before love?

2. How many rode in **The Charge of the Light Brigade**?

3. Name two poems that use animals of prey.

4. Which three poems describe a country family's response to death in war?

5. What drink is described as 'Britain's laurel-water'? Why?

6. Who would rather be a hare than a hound? Why do you think this is?

7. Name two other sounds described in **The Drum** and in **On the Idle Hill**.

8 What does Peterkin find in a field?

9 In which poem is war likened to a cricket game? Why is this?

10 What animal dies in **The Destruction of Sennacherib**?

Thinking and linking

Exam questions will ask you to write about common themes or ideas in the poems.
This activity will help you to think about the ways in which poems can be linked or
grouped together.

1 Copy and complete the chart below to show which poems, in your opinion, contain
the listed themes or ideas. The first one has been done for you.

2 Add other themes, e.g. 'Seduction' and 'Irony/satire', and complete these rows too.

Theme	Poems			
Honour and glory	The Charge of the Light Brigade	Vitaï Lampada	Ode, Written in the Beginning ...	To Lucasta ...
Death in battle				
Being a hero				
Reluctant killers				
The purpose of war				
Suffering and destruction				

3 For each poem you have chosen, select at least three quotations that help convey
the theme or idea.

4 For each quotation, add notes explaining how it helps to convey the theme or idea.
For example:

Poem: 'The Charge of the Light Brigade'

Quotation: on theme of honour and glory – 'When can their glory fade?'.

Explanation: this is a rhetorical question which does not need an
answer. It asks the reader to think about the fact that their
reputations will live forever, but we are not really supposed to question
this. Instead of a suicidal act, their actions in riding to their deaths
are described as a glorious thing.

Exploring attitudes to war

This activity will help you to:
- ✔ revise the poems in detail
- ✔ explore attitudes in the poems
- ✔ think about how imagery and language help to convey ideas
- ✔ focus on links and contrasts.

1 Test your memory of the Section by guessing which poems the quotations below come from.

- stricken mother's soul!
- The seed's a waste
- Brothers'! – children's! – parents' blood
- How sleep the brave
- And there lay the rider distorted and pale
- For many thousand bodies here/Lay rotting in the sun
- With fire and sword the country round/Was wasted far and wide
- I shot him dead because-/Because he was my foe
- The sky is shrivelled and shred
- But what good came of it at last?
- Boldly they rode and well,/Into the jaws of Death
- Take good hold in the army shirt,/And tug the corpse to light
- Loved I not honour more
- Bear through life like a torch in flame
- And mangled limbs and dying groans,/And widows' tears, and orphans' moans
- And we can range from hill to hill,/And chase our vanquished victors still
- She with thin form presently drest in black
- Yes; quaint and curious war is!

2 Check your results, especially any you are unsure of.

3 The poems in this Section are generally either pro- or anti-war. Put the quotations in a chart like the one below.

Theme	Poems
Pro-war	Anti-war
'The gleaming eagles of the legions'	'A sorry tale of sorry plans'

4 Answer the following questions or discuss them with a partner or in a group.
- **a** Which quotations were difficult to place in a column?
- **b** Which could have been put in either or both columns?
- **c** Which column had the most quotations?
- **d** How well do the pro-war and anti-war quotations group under subheadings? Are there any which do not fit?

Confidence checklist

In a chart like the one below, place a tick in the appropriate column for each statement depending on how confident you feel.

Statement	Not confident	Could do more work	Very confident
I can compare two poems that show different attitudes to town and country life.			
I can explore the way nature in the countryside is shown in two poems.			
I can discuss two poems that show a negative side of city life.			
I can explore the views of society offered in some of these poems.			
I can discuss interesting imagery in a range of poems.			
I can explore the ways in which real and ideal attitudes to the countryside are expressed.			

Re-read the poems that need more work, with your notes, highlighting what you don't understand. Discuss them with a partner or ask your teacher for help.

Memory joggers

This quiz will help you to:
- ✔ test your memory of the texts and their content
- ✔ identify which poems you may still need to work on
- ✔ think quickly and recall key details.

1. Which trees is Hopkins sad to see cut down?

2. Who thinks a view of London is the most beautiful sight on earth?

3. Describe three terrible aspects of the living conditions of a woman who sews shirts.

4. Who or what is being described in the simile 'And like a thunderbolt he falls'?

5. Name two groups of people described as suffering in Blake's **London**.

6. Who does the nymph reply to and what does she say?

7. How long ago did they shut the road through the woods?

8. Who dreams of a small cabin by a lake? Which lake?

9. Who makes a pun about a runny nose? In which poem?

10. Fill in the missing words: 'Season of ... and ... fruitfulness,/Close bosom ... of the maturing ...'

11. Name three yellow things in London that remind Oscar Wilde of the countryside.

12. Who finds dead leaves in the town unattractive?

13. In which poem is the sea described as two jewels? Which jewels?

14. How does Christina Rossetti describe the world at night? Do you think she describes the town or the countryside?

When you have finished, check your answers with your teacher or against the poems and make a note of which poems you think you need to work on more.

Remember

A poem may be read as having more than one theme or idea.

Thinking and linking

Exam questions will ask you to write about common themes or ideas in the poems. This activity will help you to think about the ways in which poems can be linked or grouped together.

1. Copy and complete the chart below to show which poems, in your opinion, contain the listed themes or ideas. The first one has been done for you.

2. Add other themes and complete these rows too.

Theme	Poems			
Suffering in the city	London	The Song of the Shirt	A Dead Harvest ...	Conveyancing
The peace of nature				
Nature in the city				
The passing of time				
Changes and seasons				
A realistic view				
An ideal view				
Beauty				

3. For each poem you have chosen, select at least three quotations that help convey the theme or idea.

4. For each quotation, add notes explaining how it helps to convey the theme or idea. For example:

◎ Extension

Create two grids –
one to show poems
which treat themes
in a similar way and
one to show those
which treat themes
in a contrasting
way.

Poem: 'London'

Quotation: suggesting theme of suffering in the city – 'In every cry of every man,/In every infant's cry of fear'.

Explanation: the repetition of 'every' in these two lines suggests how widespread the suffering is – it's not just a few people, but everyone. Including the infant crying with fear reminds the reader that the helpless and innocent suffer and are afraid in the city.

Exploring the real and the ideal

English poetry has a tradition of presenting country life as a perfect ideal. It does this through:

- description of the beauties of nature
- linking nature with innocence and happiness
- concentrating on the warm and beautiful seasons
- presenting country characters and things as attractive and simple.

1. Make a list of the town poems which present town life as a perfect ideal.

2. Complete the mindmap below to help you identify and explore the ideas on idealism in these poems.

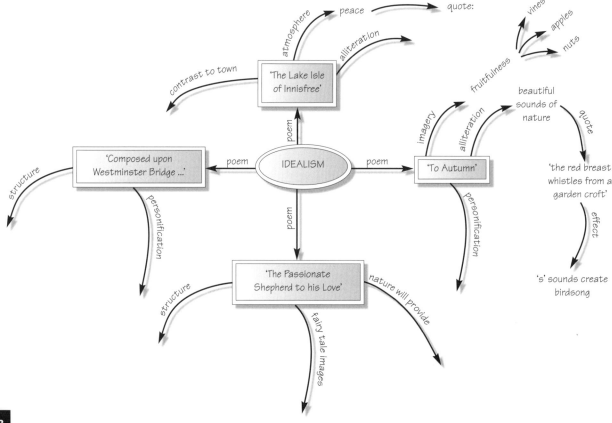

3 A range of poems in this section also presents a very real picture of life in the town or the city. What harsh realities or darker sides to life can you find in the following?
- **London**
- **The Song of the Shirt**
- **The World**
- **Binsey Poplars**
- **The Nymphs Reply ...**
- **Conveyancing**

4 Idealistic poems are written or read to escape from reality. Realistic poems are written to inform the reader about harsh truths. Does your reading of the poems make you agree or disagree with these statements?

5 Which poems seem to contain elements of both realism and idealism? How?

Exploring town and country

One obvious area to study in this section is the contrast between town and country. Some poets see beauty in towns, like Wordsworth in **Composed upon Westminster Bridge** ..., but then he is looking at London before it springs to life! Most of the poems about towns contain some criticism of town life.

1 Brainstorm your own views on the advantages and disadvantages of living in a town and living in the country. Make a chart and enter your views under the headings 'Advantages' and 'Disadvantages'.

2 Below are some images from poems about towns and about the country. Copy the chart below and fit the images in the relevant place.
- And mark in every face I meet/Marks of weakness, marks of woe
- By shallow rivers to whose falls/Melodious birds sing madrigals
- Along the graceless grass of town
- Ho! stop the thief! my handkerchief!
- That dandled a sandelled/Shadow that swam or sank
- the opal and the sapphire or that wandering western sea
- And, here and there, a passer-by/Shows like a little restless midge
- To bend with apples the mossed cottage-trees,/And fill all fruit with ripeness to the core

Quotation	Poem	How image shows criticism of towns	How image shows beauty of the country

3 Use this research to help you write a summary of:
- the qualities of the country that the poets find appealing
- the qualities of the town and the country which they dislike
- the main differences between the country and the town as expressed in the poems.

How It Looks From Here

OPENING LINES

Confidence checklist

In a chart like the one below, place a tick in the appropriate column for each statement depending on how confident you feel.

Statement	Not confident	Could do more work	Very confident
I can compare two poems that show different views of life.			
I can explore the way poets write about important memories.			
I can discuss two poems that show aspects of death.			
I can discuss the effects of structure in a range of the poems.			
I can identify and discuss two poems dealing with fear.			
I can discuss interesting imagery in a range of the poems.			
I can explore the ways in which humour is created in at least two poems.			

Re-read the poems that need more work, with your notes, highlighting what you don't understand. Discuss them with a partner or ask your teacher for help.

Memory joggers

This quiz will help you to:
- ✔ test your memory of the texts and their content
- ✔ identify which poems you may still need to work on
- ✔ think quickly and recall key details.

1. Which animal heard at night becomes a nightmare?

2. In which poem does a new bride adjust to her new life?

3. Name three qualities of the product 'life' in **A Consumer's Report**.

4. In which poem does a man watch two lovers? Why is the ending a surprise?

5. What does the grease spot left by a dead man remind Don Paterson of?

6. Who argues that poets are not given much status? Name three ways this is shown.

7. Who likens approaching death to a rugby tackle?

8. In which poem does the speaker lie awake worrying about silly things he has said or done? How does s/he use personification?

9. Name four reasons Peter Porter dislikes cats.

10. Why does Stevie Smith think we should appreciate colours?

11. Give at least two arguments that Christoper Logue uses to persuade a rat to move next door.

12. What does Sylvia Plath liken her reflection to in **Mirror**?

When you have finished, check your answers with your teacher or against the poems and make a note of which poems you think you need to work on more.

! Remember

A poem may be read as having more than one theme or idea.

Thinking and linking

Exam questions will ask you to write about common themes or ideas in the poems. This activity will help you to think about the ways in which poems can be linked or grouped together.

1. Copy and complete the chart below to show which poems, in your opinion, contain the listed themes or ideas. The first one has been done for you.

2. Add other themes and complete these rows too.

Theme	Poems			
Fears and worries	The Hare	Things	Mort aux Chats	Rat, O Rat ...
Likes and dislikes				
Life and death				
Memories				
Humour				
Night and day				
Important moments				

3. For each poem you have chosen, select at least three quotations that help convey the theme or idea.

4. For each quotation, add notes explaining how it helps to convey the theme or idea. For example:

> **Poem:** 'The Hare'
>
> **Quotation:** showing fear or worry – 'a woman shivers in her narrow bed'.
>
> **Explanation:** this quotation suggests fear and loneliness. The word 'shiver' could mean that she is scared, but also that she is cold – her 'narrow bed' tells us she is alone and has nobody to cuddle up to.

@ Extension

Create two grids – one to show poems which treat themes in a similar way and one to show those which treat themes in a contrasting way.

Looking outwards, looking inwards

These activities will help you to:
- ✔ consider different points of view in the poems
- ✔ explore links between poems in detail
- ✔ create revision aids.

Looking outwards

In this group of poems, the poets offer a view of the world and issues which affect everyone, such as the meaning of life, truth and death.

1 Complete the chart below to identify the main points the poets are making about the themes of life and death.

Poem	Life	Death
A Consumer's Report		
Defying Gravity		Takes us up out of the world
I Am a Cameraman		
Sometimes		
O Grateful Colours	Is full of colour – appreciate it	

2 Choose two of the poems which you feel offer different views and identify:
- the different views
- features of imagery, language and structure they use
- the effect they have on the reader.

Looking inwards

Some of the poems are personal reflections. The poets look inwards and describe their thoughts, feelings, worries and memories.

1 Copy the chart below and fill in the rest of the key images.

Poem	Key images	What they suggest
Mirror	'a little god'	Rules/controls the woman – it is like an altar?
Bedfellows	'His dead halo'	
Wedding Wind		
Things		
The Hare		
In Your Mind		

2 Explore the ways the images are used to convey ideas and feelings. Fill in the chart with what each image suggests.

OPENING LINES

Confidence checklist

In a chart like the one below, place a tick in the appropriate column for each statement depending on how confident you feel.

Statement	Not confident	Could do more work	Very confident
I can compare two poems that show positive and negative views of the war.			
I can explore the way women responded to the war.			
I can explore the different ways in which anger is expressed in some of the poems.			
I can discuss two poems that suggest that the war was a waste of life.			
I can compare poems which show the effects of war on the individual.			
I can discuss interesting imagery in a range of poems.			
I can explore the ways in which different attitudes to the war are shown in a range of poems.			

Re-read the poems that need more work, with your notes, highlighting what you don't understand. Discuss them with a partner or ask your teacher for help.

Memory joggers

This quiz will help you to:
- ✔ test your memory of the texts and their content
- ✔ identify which poems you may still need to work on
- ✔ think quickly and recall key details.

1. What grows between the crosses in the graveyards in Flanders?

2. Name three ways in which the Bohemians tried to rebel against army life.

3. Why do you think the survivors won't speak of the dead in **Spring Offensive**?

4. Who is angry with 'fat old men' and 'girls with feathers'? Why?

5. Who uses a parable to make a point about useless sacrifice? Why does he choose this parable and how is it different from the war?

6. In which poem does a woman still keep flowers in someone's room? Why?

7 In which poem do we see a soldier's uncontrollable grief at his brother's death?

8 Who lies to an old lady? Why? What do you think of his real opinion?

9 Who shows fear of death to be natural, not cowardly?

10 In which poem does the solider state 'Twas him or me'?

11 Which poet thinks she will never appreciate the joys of nature or be happy again?

12 Name two poems in which soldiers sing as they go off to war.

When you have finished, check your answers with your teacher or against the poems and make a note of which poems you think you need to work on more.

Thinking and linking

Exam questions will ask you to write about common themes or ideas in the poems. This activity will help you to think about the ways in which poems can be linked or grouped together.

1 Copy and complete the chart below to show which poems, in your opinion, contain the listed themes or ideas. The first one has been done for you.

2 Add other themes, e.g. 'Fear' and 'Grief and loss', and complete these rows too.

Theme	Poems			
Women at home	The Hero	The Deserter	Recruiting	Perhaps
Anger and protest				
Honour and glory				
The horrors of battle				
Effect on individuals				
Expectations and reality				

3 For each poem you have chosen, select at least three quotations that help convey the theme or idea.

4 For each quotation, add notes explaining how it helps to convey the theme or idea. For example:

Poem: The Hero

Quotation: suggesting experience of women at home – 'some gallant lies/That she would nourish all her days'.

Explanation: this suggests that the only thing mothers had to cling to was the idea that their sons had died bravely. The word 'nourish' suggests food. She will keep the idea alive, feeding it by thinking about it often, until she dies.

Exploring male and female perspectives

One way of grouping the poems is to look at those written by men, many of whom fought in the war, and those written by women, many of whom lost loved ones.

This activity will help you to:
- ✔ reflect on the different ways in which male and female poets treat the subject of war
- ✔ explore the images in some poems in detail
- ✔ develop your ideas about links and contrasts between the poems.

Doing the activity in a group with each person looking at one or two poems will help you cover all the poems and let you discuss your ideas.

1 Make a note of which poems were written by women and which by men.

2 From the poems, find quotations which suggest the images in the chart below.

Images	Quotations from poems by women	Quotations from poems by men
Soldiers going to their deaths		
Soldiers as heroes		
Soldiers as children	'With his bright eyes and cheeks all red'	
Nature	'The seed in his hand The sunny hours of spring'	
Pride		
Grief and suffering		
Time		
Fear		
Death		
Blame/anger		'Fat civilians' 'Offer the ram of pride instead'
Deceit		'Fear hushed up'

3 Copy the chart and fill in the quotations. Which images appear mostly in poems written by men or poems by women? What does this suggest about the different ways men and women saw the war and its effect on them?

4 How far do you agree that **The Deserter** is more like a poem written by a male poet? Give reasons and supporting evidence for your points.

Higher Tier, Question 1

OPENING LINES

Town and Country
- English Lit: Unit 6
- 45 mins to answer
- Choice of 3 questions
- Worth 25% of mark

Tackling the question

> What do you find interesting about the ways in which the poets write about nature and the past in **Beeny Cliff** and 'On Wenlock Edge ...'?

1 Choosing your question

When choosing your exam question, there are two things to ask yourself:
- do I understand what the question is asking me to do
- do I know enough about the texts to be able to answer the question well?

To answer this exam question, you will need to:
- ✔ be familiar with the themes of nature and the past in these poems
- ✔ feel confident that you can write about the ways the poets use language and techniques in writing about nature and the past.

Do you feel confident you can answer the question successfully? If not, look at the other questions to see if you feel more confident with them.

> ### ! Remember
>
> You will lose marks if you do not answer the question fully or if you give a partial response because you can't apply the question to the texts.

2 Planning your answer

You need to make a quick outline plan to help you structure your ideas.

a Underline the key words in the question.

> What I need to concentrate on
>
> Key ideas to concentrate on

> What do you find <u>interesting</u> about the <u>ways</u> in which the poets write about <u>nature</u> and the <u>past</u> in **Beeny Cliff** and 'On Wenlock Edge ...'?

Decide what the key words mean and think about what you are being asked to comment on. For example:
- nature and the past – why are they important; are they linked?
- Language and technique – how the poets' words, phrases and images work to suggest meaning to the reader; what is most interesting/striking about these.

> ### ! Remember
>
> Planning helps you think up and sort out your ideas and improves the structure and focus of your essays.

b Brainstorm ideas and make a few notes for each of your poems. Jot down some reminders about textual details and quotations you could use to support these points. If you prefer to plan using bullet points, look at the examples of using this technique on pages 33 and 38.

c Working from the brainstorms, decide how you would order the points. Would you write about one poem, followed by the other, or focus for example on attitude, form and then language in paragraphs on both poems? What would be the benefits and drawbacks of each approach?

Give each point on the brainstorms a number according to the order in which you would write about them. Discuss and compare your ideas with a partner.

> ### ☀ Top tip
>
> Use your plan to keep your answer on track.

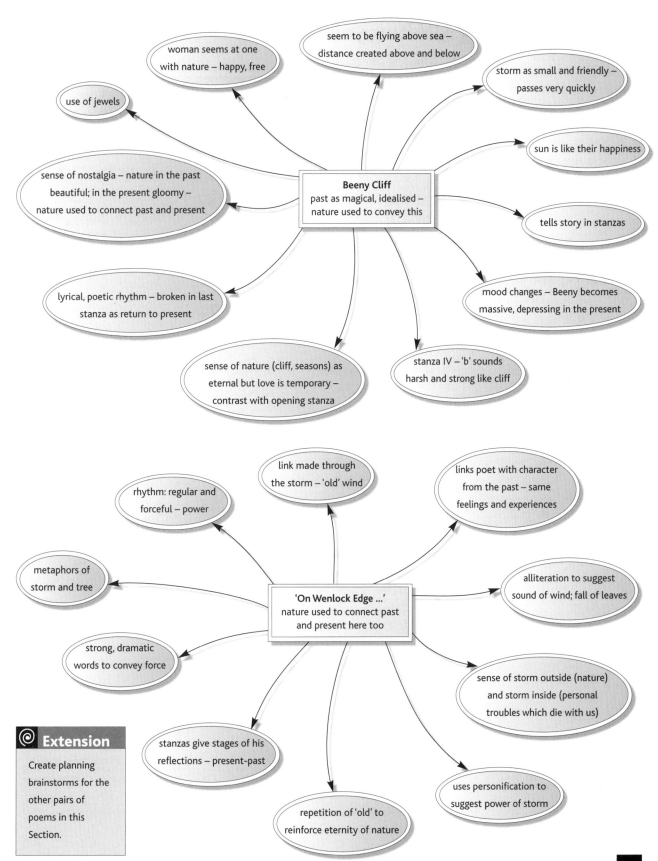

woman seems at one with nature – happy, free

seem to be flying above sea – distance created above and below

storm as small and friendly – passes very quickly

use of jewels

sun is like their happiness

sense of nostalgia – nature in the past beautiful; in the present gloomy – nature used to connect past and present

Beeny Cliff
past as magical, idealised – nature used to convey this

tells story in stanzas

lyrical, poetic rhythm – broken in last stanza as return to present

mood changes – Beeny becomes massive, depressing in the present

sense of nature (cliff, seasons) as eternal but love is temporary – contrast with opening stanza

stanza IV – 'b' sounds harsh and strong like cliff

link made through the storm – 'old' wind

links poet with character from the past – same feelings and experiences

rhythm: regular and forceful – power

metaphors of storm and tree

'On Wenlock Edge ...'
nature used to connect past and present here too

alliteration to suggest sound of wind; fall of leaves

strong, dramatic words to convey force

sense of storm outside (nature) and storm inside (personal troubles which die with us)

stanzas give stages of his reflections – present-past

uses personification to suggest power of storm

repetition of 'old' to reinforce eternity of nature

@ **Extension**

Create planning brainstorms for the other pairs of poems in this Section.

3 Writing your answer

a Opening paragraph

First, introduce both of your poems and the aspect of the ending of relationships that each deals with. Don't state the obvious, for example: '*I am going to write about …*'. Start your answer with a crisper first sentence and then give a brief overview in one or two more sentences. For example:

> In the poems 'Beeny Cliff' and 'On Wenlock Edge …' both poets are inspired by nature to reflect on the past. In 'Beeny Cliff' the landscape evokes memories of the freedom and passion of young love and contrasts it with the present in which only the cliff is the same, whereas the storm in 'On Wenlock Edge …' leads the poet to reflect on the temporary nature of life compared with the permanence of nature.

b Following paragraphs

Use the guidelines on page 77 to unite the main part of your answer. Remember to use the three-point formula, for example:

Respond → When Hardy moves to the present in stanza IV the image of nature changes and becomes darker.

Quote → He describes how the 'chasmal beauty bulks old Beeny to the sky'.

Comment → The language in this line works to suggest something powerful and massive. The beauty is 'chasmal' now, suggesting deep, dark chasms. The alliteration of the 'b' sounds adds hardness and the word 'bulks' makes me think of something massive and indestructible. This contrasts with the beauty of nature remembered from the past, and the temporariness of the woman's love. Unlike her promises, we get the idea that Beeny cliff will last.

Top tips

- Check that your 'comments' are the longest parts of your paragraphs. If they aren't, spend more time developing your ideas.
- Make sure your 'comment' is focused on details such as the language which shows how the poet is suggesting ideas, and is not just a repeat of your 'respond' point. Try focusing on one or two words from your quotation and broaden out your comments from there.
- It's better to say a lot about a little, not the other way round. You cannot say everything that could be said about the poems, so aim to write about two or three things in detail.

c **Final paragraph**

Write your conclusion using the guidelines on page 78. Try to offer a personal response, for example saying which poem you found most effective and why:

> In both of the poems, nature seems to evoke a melancholy feeling. Both poets reflect on the temporary nature of experience — reading the poems made me feel how weak we and our feelings are.

 4 Writing your answer

Errors cost marks take the time to check the aspects listed on page 45.

Looking at candidates' answers

Using your own experience, and the guidance offered so far, what advice would you give to each of these students, based on these extracts from their answers?

Noel

'Beeny Cliff' starts with a romantic idea of the past as a time of freedom and brightness. The sea is made of opals and sapphires and the image of the woman 'riding high above' could be a metaphor for riding high in life as well as literally describing someone riding a horse on a cliff. Her 'bright hair' links her with nature, with the jewel images and makes the past seem bright and special in his memory. It was also a time of freedom — her hair is 'flapping free' and this poem was written at a time when women wore their hair up so it could suggest freedom from the rules in the past when they were young. This is a contrast to 'On Wenlock Edge' which starts in the present with a description of a storm. The language suggests the power of the storm with words like 'heaves' and Housman describes how the wind 'bends the saplings double'. His picture of nature is of a powerful and destructive force which batters the woods. The link with the past is made clear as the poet moves on to the next stanzas and describes how the same wind blew in olden days.

Kreso

Both the poets use storms in their poems. In 'On Wenlock Edge ...' the storm makes him think about the past. He imagines a Roman from the old city of Uricon standing where he is, having the same thoughts as him. The storm turns into a metaphor as the poem goes on. This is interesting because in the first stanza he describes how the storm damages the woods. This shows that life is hard and it will hurt us and it has always been the same. The storm makes him think of this because nature is always the same in the past and in the present. Hardy also uses a storm in 'Beeny Cliff' but his storm is only temporary and is part of the beauty of nature. The cloud is 'little' showing it is not dangerous and the rain is 'irised' which is a beautiful flower. This shows the storm is beautiful and not frightening. I think the storm here could be like the lovers having an argument that blows over quickly and does not spoil their day — the sun comes out again quickly. In this poem a storm does not make him think of the past because the weather is temporary.

Examiner's comments

Noel starts well with a point that links to the essay question. He uses quotation efficiently – he simply makes close reference to the jewels because this is not the part he wants to explore in most depth. He uses an actual quotation for his next sentence, because he wants to explore this in more detail. He uses a technical term, metaphor, and doesn't just identify it, but considers how it adds to the poem.

The next comment about women's hair makes a link to the historical context and picks up marks for him. He moves on to discuss the opening of the next poem, showing he is structuring his essay well, not just writing two mini-essays on the poems. He quickly focuses on language – although he could make more of the strong visual and aural images in this stanza.

Overall, Noel explores language and technique with confidence. He knows the poems well and knows what he wants to say about them. He keeps a focus on the exam question, and works in his understanding of context and technique. He should include a range of points about different techniques in his planning stage. If he manages to do this, he is heading for a top grade. Working to Grade A.

Kreso also clearly knows and understands the poems. He starts with a comparative point, although he could phrase it to link with the question more closely, for example: 'An aspect of nature which both poets use to reflect on the past is a storm'.

Kreso then makes the mistake of summarising the poem rather than exploring. He doesn't tell how the Roman is described or why it is important. He mentions that the storm is used as a metaphor, but he does not quote and comment on the metaphor. He does, however, make a good link to the opening of the poem and shows why the idea is interesting – although, again, with no quotation or close exploration of language.

Like Noel, he moves on to discuss the use of storm imagery in the next poem. This shows that he too is structuring his essay carefully and probably took time to plan. His writing about this poem is more successful because he quotes words and explains their importance and what they suggest. Although he quotes only single words, these are well integrated into his sentences. He has explored the idea of what the storm represents well in this paragraph, although he has missed the opportunity to comment on the other features, such as alliteration, used to describe it.

Kreso should make sure that he thinks about how he is going to use quotation and possibly underline key words and phrases in the text in the planning stages. At present Kreso's understanding seems better than his essay technique. If he wants his grade to reflect how well he knows and appreciates the poems, he needs to work on building detail into his work, rather than summarising. At the moment, he is failing to meet the criteria for the highest marks. Working to Grade B.

Higher Tier, Question 2
OPENING LINES

1914–1918 War (ii)
- English Lit: Unit 2
- 45 mins to answer
- Choice of 3 questions
- Worth 25% of mark

Tackling the question

Compare the ways in which the poets present the relationship between the young and the old and express feelings about war in these two poems.

The Seed-Merchant's Son by Agnes Grozier Herbertson

The <u>Seed-Merchant</u> has lost his son,
<u>His dear, his loved, his only</u> one.

> Significance of father's job?

> Repetition?

<u>So young</u> he was. Even now it seems
He was <u>a child</u> with a child's dreams.

5 He would <u>race</u> over the meadow-bed
With his bright, <u>bright eyes and his cheeks all red.</u>

<u>Fair and healthy</u> and long of limb:
It made one young just to look at him.

> Underlined phrases: emphasis on youth – health, colour, movement, energy, innocence.

His school books, into the cupboard thrust,
10 Have scarcely had time to gather dust.

Died in the war … And it seems his eyes
Must have looked at death with a <u>child's surprise</u>.

The Seed-Merchant goes on his way:
<u>I saw</u> him out on his land today;

> Use of observer/narrator and on line 26.

15 <u>Old to have fathered so young</u> a <u>son</u>,
And now the <u>last glint of his youth</u> is <u>gone</u>.

> Introduces age/youth contrast.

> The only weak rhyme in couplet structures.

What could one say to him in his need?
Little there seemed to say indeed.

> Age – father – colourless, lifeless, motionless – effect of grief - contrast with description of son.

<u>So still</u> he was that the birds flew round
20 The <u>grey</u> of his head without a sound,

Careless and tranquil in the air,
As if <u>naught human</u> were standing there.

Oh, never a soul could understand
Why he looked at the earth, and <u>the seed</u> in his hand,

> Tacked-on final section – strange twist; mystery – observer doesn't understand why the father thanks God – some hope at the end?

> Symbols of renewal, life carrying on?

25 As he had never before seen <u>seed</u> or sod:
<u>I heard</u> him murmur: 'Thank God, thank God!'

> Enjambment, alliteration – rhythm breaking down, difficult line to say.

The Parable of the Old Man and the Young
by Wilfred Owen

So Abram rose, and <u>clave</u> the wood, and went,
And took the fire with him, and a knife.
And as they sojourned both of them together,
Isaac the first-born <u>spake</u> and said, My Father,
5 Behold the preparations, fire and iron,
But <u>where</u> the <u>lamb</u>, for this burnt offering?
Then Abram <u>bound the youth with belts and straps</u>,
And builded <u>parapets and trenches</u> there,
And stretched forth the knife to slay his son.
10 When <u>lo</u>! an Angel called him out of heaven,
Saying, Lay not thy hand upon the lad,
Neither do anything to him, thy son.
Behold! Caught in a thicket by its horns,
A Ram. Offer the <u>Ram of Pride</u> instead.
15 But the old man would not <u>so</u>, <u>but slew his son</u>,
And half the <u>seed</u> of Europe, one by one.

Annotations (left):

Questions of son, Isaac's confusion and innocence.

Wordplay on so/sow – this Abram and old war leaders don't sow seeds but destroy them (Isaac and soldiers).

Final rhyming couplet, changes sonnet structure and bible story – bitter, ironic attack on the old sacrificing the young in the Great War.

Annotations (right):

Biblical language, reminders of bible story and its happy ending (and line 10).

Strong alliteration – young controlled by the old – army equipment.

Language of War – Abram = war leaders/statesmen forcing young men to war?

Capital letters – pride personified as ram – pride/stubbornness of old men sacrificing young men?

Alliteration and breakdown in rhythm – violent/surprising change to bible story – Abram not father of a race here but destroyer.

1 Choosing your question

When choosing your exam question, there are two things to ask yourself:
* do I understand what the question is asking me to do
* do I know enough about the texts to be able to answer the question well?

To answer this exam question, you will need to:
✔ identify some similarities and differences between the two poems
✔ identify the relationship between the young and the old in each poem
✔ identify some feelings about war in each poem
✔ identify some key words which make these feelings clear.

Do you feel confident you can answer the question successfully? If not, look at the other questions to see if you feel more confident with them.

! Remember

You will lose marks if you do not answer the question fully or if you give a partial response because you can't apply the question to the texts.

2 Planning your answer

You need to make a quick outline plan to help you structure your ideas.

a   Underline the key words in the question.

> <u>Compare the ways</u> in which the poets present the relationship between <u>the young and the old</u> and express <u>feelings about war</u> in these two poems.

Decide what the key words mean and think about what you are being asked to comment on:
* the relationship between young and old
* the expression of feelings about war.

b Annotating the poems will help you form some ideas about the ways in which the poems are similar in some ways and different in others. One candidate's notes have been added to the poems in the question as an example. Re-read the two poems and the annotations and think about:
- why these parts have been picked out
- how the notes relate to the question
- what extra notes you would add.

c Comparing the poems in a chart like the one below is one way of seeing the similarities and differences clearly. This is a good idea for revision, even though you will not have time to make a chart in the exam.
Tick the ideas which seem important enough to use in your essay. Add other ideas of your own.

Similarities	Differences
• about the death of young men in war	• grief (Herbertson) – anger (Owen)
• twists or changes at the end	• bitter attack on the father/the old (O) – sympathy for father (H)
• images of sowing and destroying seeds	• full, personal descriptions of father and son (H) – Abram and Isaac used more as symbolic figures (O)
• opening rhyme (Herbertson); closing rhyme (Owen) – exactly the same	• Herbertson a woman – Owen a man

d Decide on how you would order the points. After a brief introduction, you might discuss **The Seed-Merchant's Son** first. Then you could discuss **The Parable ...**, referring back to **The Seed-Merchant's Son** to point out any similarities and differences between the two poems. Linking words/phrases like 'also', 'similarly', 'in the same way', and 'as' for similarities and 'unlike', 'in contrast to' and 'on the other hand' for differences will help to shape your comparison.
Give each point a number according to the order in which you would write about them.

⏱ 30 MINS 3 Writing your answer

a Opening paragraph

Write your opening paragraph, using the following guidelines.

✔ First, introduce both of your poems focusing on the words in the question.

✔ Briefly introduce the different situations in each poem: the merchant's loss of his only son and the adaptation of the bible story

✔ Briefly suggest some general similarities and differences in the feelings about war and the relationship between young and old in each poem.

b Following paragraphs

Use the guidelines given on page 77 to write the main part of your answer.

Look at the following two extracts taken from the middle sections of two candidates' answers. Who is going to get a higher mark?

Kim

'The Seed Merchant's Son' is written in rhyming couplets whereas 'The Parable of the Old Man and the Young' is a sonnet with a rhyming couplet added on to the end. Owen uses iambic pentameter but breaks this rhythm down in the penultimate line. Herbertson uses iambic tetrameter rhythm and she breaks it down in her penultimate line as well. Both poets use seed imagery and alliteration to bring their poems to an end.

Sarfraz

Owen does not spend as much time building up a contrast between the young and the old, but develops the Abram and Isaac bible story in a way that relates to the Great War and shows that the young are (like lambs to the slaughter) sacrificed by the old. Owen begins to move away from the original story when he introduces 'fire and iron' and the 'parapets and trenches' which suggest the battlefield. Abram's binding of his son with 'belts and straps' (of an army uniform) symbolises to me the forcing of the younger generation into the army by an older generation of politicians and leaders determined to fight a war.

Examiner's comments

Kim is obviously a bright student who can correctly identify a whole range of technical features but there is very little to reward here. She is trying hard to compare the poems, but she swings so quickly from one to the other that she is unable to say anything worthwhile about the relationships between young and old or the attitudes to war. In other words she is not answering the question or getting to the heart of either poem.

Sarfraz begins with a reference to 'The Seed Merchant ...' which he has already discussed and he suggests a difference between the two poems. He fits well-selected quotations into his discussion, shows sharp understanding of the poem and really tackles the question. He uses the three-point formula and shows some awareness of the poets and their techniques (contrast, bible story, symbolism). Writing like this should bring him a top grade overall.

The three following candidates all wrote about the ending of '**The Parable ...**' trying to use the three point formula. Decide which candidate:

- spent the most time on the comment stage, and got the highest mark
- tried to comment on the language but was rather vague
- missed out the comment stage completely?

Joe

At the end of the poem the old man 'slew his son'.

Thomas

It's a great shock when Owen changes the bible story with the words 'slew his son'. The alliteration makes the ending of the poem very vivid and really helps you to picture the scene and understand what Owen is trying to say.

Meimee

Owen increases the shock of the ending by setting the final rhyming couplet (and the poem's only strong rhyme) apart from the rest of the poem's sonnet-like structure. This emphasises the change from the bible story and the stupidity of an older generation prepared to sacrifice their young as 'burnt offerings'. Owen uses the image of young people as 'seed' that will never grow because of the decisions of their elders. His contempt for the 'old man' and others like him comes through the hissing alliteration of the last two lines.

---

c   Final paragraph

Write your conclusion to the question using the guidelines on page 78.

4 Checking your answer

Errors cost marks so take the time to check the aspects listed on page 78:

- ✔ written expression.
- ✔ spelling of the names of the authors and the characters.
- ✔ other slips of the pen such as punctuation problems or words missed out.
- ✔ add any afterthoughts that occur to you as you read through to the end of the answer and indicate clearly, using an asterisk, numbers or letters, where they should be included.

! Remember

It's ok if your ideas about the feelings in the poems are different from those here. The examiner is genuinely interested in what you think, not expecting one 'right' answer.

War
- English Lit: Unit 6
- 45 mins to answer
- Choice of 3 questions
- Worth 25% of mark

Tackling the question

> How are feelings about war communicated to you by the poets in **Vitaï Lampada** and **The Man He Killed?**

 2 MINS

1 Choosing your question

When choosing your exam question, there are two things to ask yourself:
- do I understand what the question is asking me to do
- do I know enough about the texts to be able to answer the question well?

Do you feel confident you can answer the question successfully? If not, look at the other questions to see if you feel more confident with them.

 10 MINS

2 Planning your answer

You need to make a quick outline plan to help you structure your ideas.

a   Underline the key words in the question.

Need to show how they do this

Focus of my points

> How are <u>feelings about war communicated</u> to you by the poets in **Vitaï Lampada** and **The Man He Killed**?

Decide what the key words mean and think about what you are being asked to comment on, for example:
- feelings about war
- the poets' communication – the words and phrases, how feelings about war are suggested
- technique – other interesting aspects of the poem such as form, imagery and pace.

As you skim the poems, make a note of words and phrases that communicate feelings about war.

b   Brainstorm ideas and make a few notes for each of your poems. Jot down some reminders about textual details and quotations you could use to support these points.

If you prefer to plan using bullet points, look at the examples of using this technique on pages 33 and 38.

c   Working from the brainstorms, decide how you would order the points. Would you write about one poem, followed by the other, or focus for example on attitude, form and then language in paragraphs on both poems? What would be the benefits and drawbacks of each approach?
Give each point on the brainstorms a number according to the order in which you would write about them. Discuss your thoughts with a partner.

! Remember

You will lose marks if you do not answer the question fully or if you give a partial response because you can't apply the question to the texts.

! Remember

Planning helps you think up and sort out your ideas and improves the structure and focus of your essays.

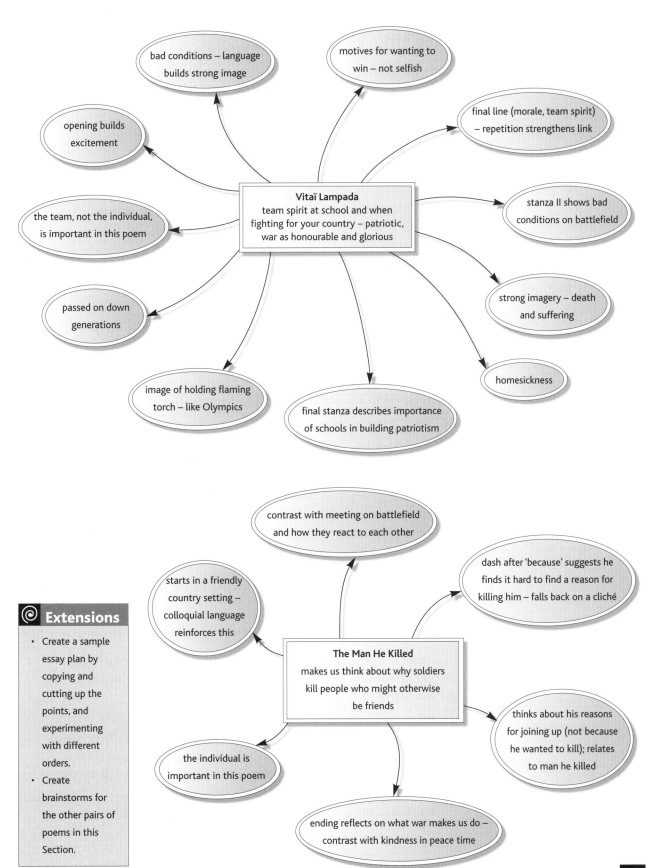

bad conditions – language builds strong image

motives for wanting to win – not selfish

final line (morale, team spirit) – repetition strengthens link

opening builds excitement

Vitaï Lampada
team spirit at school and when fighting for your country – patriotic, war as honourable and glorious

stanza II shows bad conditions on battlefield

the team, not the individual, is important in this poem

strong imagery – death and suffering

passed on down generations

homesickness

image of holding flaming torch – like Olympics

final stanza describes importance of schools in building patriotism

contrast with meeting on battlefield and how they react to each other

starts in a friendly country setting – colloquial language reinforces this

dash after 'because' suggests he finds it hard to find a reason for killing him – falls back on a cliché

The Man He Killed
makes us think about why soldiers kill people who might otherwise be friends

the individual is important in this poem

thinks about his reasons for joining up (not because he wanted to kill); relates to man he killed

ending reflects on what war makes us do – contrast with kindness in peace time

@ **Extensions**

- Create a sample essay plan by copying and cutting up the points, and experimenting with different orders.
- Create brainstorms for the other pairs of poems in this Section.

Top tip

Use your plan to keep your answer on track.

 3 Writing your answer

a Opening paragraph

Before writing your own opening paragraph, look at the two answers from other candidates below. Decide how successful each candidate has been and what each could do to improve.

Rhiannon

I am writing about 'Vitaï Lampada' and 'the Man He Killed'. 'Vitaï Lampada' is about a person who was in the war to win whereas 'The Man he Killed' is about a man who has no choice to be in the war he is there because he has no job. Both are about war, death and killing but they are different in many ways.

Stephen

In both of the poems the poets explain about war and death. In 'Vitaï Lampada' they are comparing it to a cricket game and are out to win. The poet says things like 'Ten to make and the match to win'.

Examiner's comments

Remember

An introduction shows the examiner your overall approach and guides them into what you think about the poems.

Rhiannon wastes time by starting with 'I am going to write about ...'. Not advisable, especially as the poems are chosen in the question. She does well to open with a summary of the poems, but she does not need to say the 'they are different in many ways' – she would do better to say that they show different feelings about war – this would focus on the question more strongly. She uses a good comparative word, 'whereas', to connect her ideas.

Stephen makes the mistake of launching into the detail of one poem in his introduction. After his sentence summarising 'Vitaï Lampada' he should write another sentence summarising 'The Man He Killed' in the same way to make this an effective introduction.

Now write an opening paragraph yourself. First, introduce both of your poems and the feelings about war that each communicates. Then, in one or two sentences, give a brief overview.

Top tip

Keep introductions brief and clear; leave the detail to the main part of your answer.

b Following paragraphs

Use the guidelines given on page 77 to write the main part of your answer. On page 73 there are some more examples of candidates' work on this question. For each of the examples, decide if they have followed the three-point formula and how their paragraphs could be improved.

Take one of the answers and re-write it, using the three-point formula.

Elisha

In 'Vitaï Lampada' the war is compared to a cricket game. The men take a phrase away with them from public school to war, 'Play up, play up and play the game'. This is repeated throughout the poem at the end of each stanza. The repetition makes you realise the war is compared to a cricket match.

Razwan

'The Man He Killed' is about fighting your enemy. You are stood face to face and you kill the enemy opposite you. But it is also saying that if you didn't shoot him in normal times you'd be in the pub buying him a drink or you'd lend him some money.

Examiner's comments

Elisha's work follows the guidelines, and she has made a successful comment about how something is suggested in the poem. She does not just say that there is repetition, she describes its effect in the poem. She could improve by making the point clearer at the start – it is not clear until the end that the technique she is writing about is repetition.

She should begin the point by saying 'the poet uses repetition to link public school and war'. Working towards Grade C.

Razwan clearly understands what the poem is about, but he has summarised it instead of explaining where and how we get the ideas. He has not used any quotation and has not explored the poem in detail. This paragraph is Respond – Respond – Respond. Working towards Grade F.

c   Final paragraph
Write your conclusion to the question using the guidelines on page 78. Try to offer a personal response, for example:

'Vitaï Lampada' helped me to understand why some soldiers sacrifice themselves, especially if team spirit has been drummed into them from school. 'The Man He Killed' made me think about what it might be like to be in a 'kill or be killed' situation, especially if the enemy seemed just like me, someone who might otherwise have been a friend.

 4 Checking your answer

Errors cost marks so take time to check the aspects listed on page 78.

> **! Remember**
>
> It's ok if your ideas about the feelings in the poems are different from those here. The examiner is genuinely interested in what you think, not expecting one 'right' answer.

Foundation Tier, Question 4

OPENING LINES

How It Looks From Here

• English Lit: Unit 2

• 45 mins to answer

• Choice of 3 questions

• Worth 25% of mark

Tackling the question

In **Bedfellows** and **Defying Gravity**, Don Paterson and Roger McGough reflect on a person's death. What feelings do they express and how do they make these feelings clear to you?

 1 Choosing your question

When choosing your exam question, there are two things to ask yourself:
• do I understand what the question is asking me to do
• do I know enough about the texts to be able to answer the question well?

To answer this exam question, you will need to:
✔ see some feelings about death in each poem
✔ see some key words which make these feelings clear
✔ understand the poems' difficult words like 'innuendo' and 'inoperable'.

Do you feel confident you can answer the question successfully? If not, look at the other questions to see if you feel more confident with them.

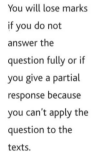

! Remember

You will lose marks if you do not answer the question fully or if you give a partial response because you can't apply the question to the texts.

 2 Planning your answer

You need to make a quick outline plan to help you structure your ideas.

a Underline the key words in the question.

In **Bedfellows** and **Defying Gravity**, Don Paterson and Roger McGough reflect on <u>a person's death</u>. What <u>feelings</u> do they express and <u>how</u> do they make these feelings clear to you?

Top tip

It can be helpful to put the question to yourself in different ways, for example:
• what are the poets' reactions to death?
• how do the poets put across their feelings about death in a striking way (words, images, structure)?

Decide what the key words mean and think about what you are being asked to comment on: the person's death and the expression of feelings.

An example of one candidate's notes have been given on the poem on page 74. Look at the notes and think about:
✔ why these parts of the poems have been picked out
✔ how the notes relate to the question
✔ what notes you might make.

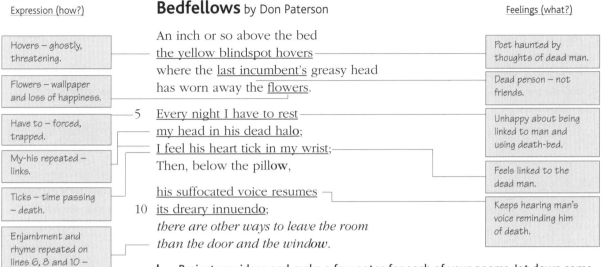

Expression (how?)

Hovers – ghostly, threatening.	
Flowers – wallpaper and loss of happiness.	
Have to – forced, trapped.	
My–his repeated – links.	
Ticks – time passing – death.	
Enjambment and rhyme repeated on lines 6, 8 and 10 – can't escape depressing message that he will also die one day.	

Bedfellows by Don Paterson

An inch or so above the bed
the yellow blindspot hovers
where the last incumbent's greasy head
has worn away the flowers.

5 Every night I have to rest
my head in his dead halo;
I feel his heart tick in my wrist;
Then, below the pillow,

his suffocated voice resumes
10 its dreary innuendo;
there are other ways to leave the room
than the door and the window.

Feelings (what?)

Poet haunted by thoughts of dead man.	
Dead person – not friends.	
Unhappy about being linked to man and using death-bed.	
Feels linked to the dead man.	
Keeps hearing man's voice reminding him of death.	

b Brainstorm ideas and make a few notes for each of your poems. Jot down some reminders about textual details and quotations you could use to support these points. If you prefer to plan using bullet points, look at the examples of using this technique on pages 33 and 38.

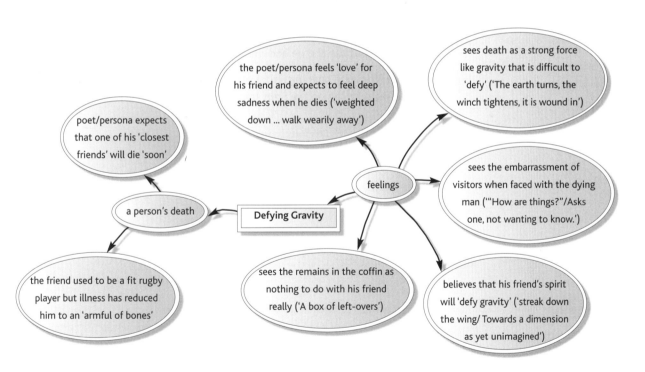

Look closely at the quotations picked out from **Bedfellows** and **Defying Gravity**. What can you find to say about the words themselves and the ways in which the poets have put across their feelings about death?

Remember

Planning helps you think up and sort out your ideas and improves the structure and focus of your essays.

c   Working from the brainstorms, decide how you would order the points. Remember that it is important to write about one poem and then the other, pointing out similarities and differences as you go along. What would be the benefits and drawbacks of each approach?

Give each point on the brainstorms a number according to the order in which you would write about them. Discuss and compare your ideas with a partner.

 Top tips

- Use your plan to keep your answer on track.
- Foundation Tier questions often have a 'what' part on the ideas and feelings in the poems, and a 'how' part on the language and structure. Don't write about the two separately, but if you focus more closely on the words and shape of the poems as you write about the ideas, you will be highly rewarded.

Remember

An introduction shows the examiner your overall approach and guides them into what you think about the poems.

3 Writing your answer

a   **Opening paragraph**

Write your opening paragraph, using the following guidelines.
- ✔ First, introduce both of your poems focusing on the words in the question.
- ✔ Then, in one or two sentences, give a brief overview of some of the general feelings about the theme and the situation in each poem.

Look at the following openings from other candidates' answers. Which candidate seems to be on the right track?

> Kim
>
> I am going to write about the feelings about death in 'Bedfellows' and 'Defying Gravity' and about how these feelings are made clear to me.

Top tip

Keep introductions brief and clear; leave the detail to the main part of your answer.

> Zoe
>
> In the first stanza of 'Bedfellows', Paterson describes the way the flowery wallpaper above his bed has been worn away by the head of the last person who slept (and probably died) there. Paterson is aware of the presence of the dead man and thinks that he hears his voice telling him that there are other ways to leave the room apart from the door or the window. What the poet is trying to say, is that he could leave the room by dying as well.

Ifeoma

In 'Bedfellows', Don Paterson imagines himself using the bed of a man who has died. He feels haunted by the presence of the dead man but is really sorry for himself, not the man, because he feels he is doomed to share the same fate. Unlike Paterson, Roger McGough is not really concerned about himself but about a close friend who is dying from a serious illness. In this poem too there is a feeling of doom that death is a force like gravity which affects us all.

Examiner's comments

Kim wastes time announcing what she's going to do. You can see that she's trying hard to focus on the wording of the question but she's just repeating it and not saying anything new.

Zoe certainly shows a confident understanding of 'Bedfellows' but she is not introducing both poems and she is not answering the question. Her approach is to work through one poem and to explain what it means to her rather than to focus on the question and the 'feelings about death' in both poems. Her comment 'What the poet is trying to say' sounds as if she doesn't like poetry much and would prefer plain ideas in plain language.

Ifeoma is a star! You might not agree with everything she says. For example, is there something amusing and almost lighthearted about both poems rather than sad and doom-laden? But she introduces the 'dead person' in each poem and brings out 'feelings about death' as well as some similarities and differences between the poems. It doesn't matter that she hasn't looked closely at language yet. That can happen as she develops these ideas throughout the essay, using the three-point formula.

b **Following paragraphs**

Use the following guidelines to write the main part of your answer.

✔ Keep the question in view and in mind throughout.

✔ Follow your plan of the points you are going to make and the order in which you are going to deal with them.

✔ Start each new paragraph with a point which clearly relates to the question.

✔ Use the writers' names and focus on the techniques they use rather than just telling the story.

✔ Use the three-point formula, for example:

Respond	► McGough believes that his friend's spirit will defy gravity and …
Quote	► … 'streak down the wing/Towards a dimension as yet unimagined'.
	The rugby metaphor has a sad effect in one way because it reminds me of when the friend was fit, strong and healthy but it also suggests that
Comment	► McGough feels that death does not tie his friend to the earth but allows him to escape from his illness and run free again. The word 'wing' even has a feeling of angels about it as well as rugby so that the feeling about death here is not a sad one.

! Remember

It's ok if your ideas about the feelings in the poems are different from those here. The examiner is genuinely interested in what you think, not expecting one 'right' answer.

☆ Top tips

- Check that your 'comments' are the longest parts of your paragraphs. If they aren't, spend more time developing your ideas.
- Make sure your 'comment' is focused on details such as the language which shows how the poet is suggesting ideas, and is not just a repeat of your 'respond' point. Try focusing on one or two words from your quotation and broaden out your comments from there.
- It's better to say a lot about a little, not the other way round. You cannot say everything that could be said about the poems, so aim to write about two or three things in detail.

c **Final paragraph**
Write your conclusion to the question using the guidelines below.
✔ Refer to both poems.
✔ Try to offer a fresh perspective so you are not just summing up and repeating yourself, perhaps about the way the poems end.
✔ Try to offer a personal response. You could explain:
   – which poem you found most effective and why
   – which aspects of the poems you feel are the most interesting
   – which poem is closest to your own views or feelings
   – how a poem offers you new ideas or views of something you might not have thought about before.

🕮 4 Checking your answer

Errors cost marks so it is worth taking the time to check:
✔ written expression
✔ spelling of the names of the authors and the characters
✔ other slips of the pen such as punctuation problems or words missed out
✔ add any afterthoughts that occur to you as you read through to the end of the answer and indicate clearly, using an asterisk, numbers or letters, where they should be included.

Stories for examination in
2003–2008

Active revision

OPENING WORLDS

Thinking and Linking

Every exam question that you tackle on the **Opening Worlds** story collection will require you to write about the links between two stories. A clear picture in your mind of how the stories could be grouped together is therefore vital for your revision work. The following activity will help you to group the stories according to particular themes and see the links between them.

Concept map for themes

1. Copy the chart below on a large sheet of paper allowing plenty of space to add more columns.

2. Tick the appropriate columns to show which stories bring out the themes listed across the top. The theme on childhood has been done for you.

3. Decide how and where each theme is brought out in the stories you choose.

4. Add more themes across the top and fill in the columns for them as well.

	Culture clash	Poverty	Parents/ children	Injustice	School	Childhood	Sense of belonging
Dead Men's Path							
Snapshots of a Wedding							
The Train from Rhodesia							
The Gold-Legged Frog							
Two Kinds						✔	
The Tall Woman and Her Short Husband							
The Pieces of Silver						✔	
The Red Ball						✔	
The Young Couple							
Leela's Friend						✔	
Games at Twilight						✔	
The Winter Oak						✔	

Chinua Achebe

OPENING WORLDS

Dead Men's Path

Memory joggers

Try the first three activities below without looking at the text.

What happens

Test your memory of what happens in the story by answering the following questions.

1. How old is Michael Obi?

2. What are his two aims for the school?

3. Why is the path important to the village people?

4. Why does Obi refuse to re-open the path?

Character checks and relationships reminders

What memories about the main characters and the development of the story do the following items bring to mind:

- Obi's 'deep-set eyes'
- Nancy's magazine
- barbed wire
- a walking-stick
- the death of a 'young woman'?

Quotation quiz

1. Try to fill in the gaps in these quotations from memory and then decide who says each one, to whom, when, about what and why the quotation is important in the story. The first one has been done for you.

> a   'It had always been an <u>unprogressive</u> school ...'
> b   '... she had become completely infected by his passion for _____ _____ ...'
> c   '"The whole purpose of our school ... is to _____ just such beliefs as that."'
> d   '"let the _____ perch and let the _____ perch."'
> e   '"... the misguided _____ of the new headmaster."'
>
> The first quotation is a direct comment from Achebe giving the reader important background information at the start of the story and setting up the conflict, between tradition and change, to come. He suggests that the school is rather backward and unadventurous in its methods, and that Obi has been selected to shake it up.

Now go back to the story and check all your answers against the details in the story.

Revisiting the text

The next three activities all require close attention to the text.

Get the characters and conflicts covered

The quotations in the quiz should remind you about the three main characters: Obi, Nancy and the village priest.

1 Underline the quotations in the text and write some notes on what you think each one shows about the characters, the ways Achebe presents them to us and the conflicts between them.

2 Choose some more brief quotations for Obi, Nancy and the village priest. Underline the new quotations and write more notes as before.

Thinking and linking

Look at the following thematic headings:

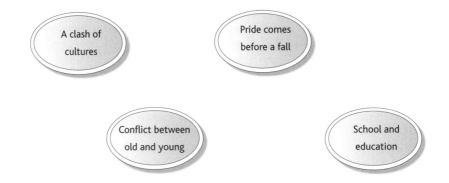

A clash of cultures

Pride comes before a fall

Conflict between old and young

School and education

For each of them decide on:
- the moment in the story when you feel Achebe brings out the theme most strongly
- two other stories in **Opening Worlds** which you feel also bring out this theme.

Looking at language

Focus on the following extract and try to explain as fully as possible how the language Achebe has chosen brings out some of the story's central ideas. Use the key terms.

Beautiful hibiscus and allamanda hedges in brilliant red and yellow marked out the carefully tended school compound from the rank neighbourhood bushes. **(lines 49–51)**

Extension

At the end of the story we are given an extract from the 'nasty report' which the Supervisor writes after inspecting the school. Put yourself in the position of the Supervisor and write the report.

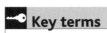 **Key terms**

- symbolism
- setting
- contrast
- antithesis
- imagery
- alliteration
- adjectives

Bessie Head

OPENING WORLDS

Snapshots of a Wedding

Memory joggers

Try the first three activities below without looking at the text.

What happens

Test your memory of what happens in the story by answering the following questions.

1. What makes Neo different from all her family?

2. Why is she unpopular and disliked even by her own relatives?

3. What does Neo's aunt say to her and what effect does this have?

Character checks and relationships reminders

What memories about the main characters and the development of the story do the following items bring to mind:
- the present of an ox
- maintenance payments of R10.00 a month
- a promise to supply water and a promise to supply corn
- a hoe, a shawl and a kerchief?

Quotation quiz

1. Try to fill in the gaps in these quotations from memory and then decide who says each one, to whom, when, about what and why the quotation is important in the story. The second one has been done for you.

> a   "'This is going to be a _____ wedding.'"
>
> b   '... she was an impossible girl with haughty, <u>arrogant</u> ways.'
>
> c   "'He is of course just running after the _____ and not the manners ...'"
>
> d   '... he would sit ... turn his head sideways and stare at what seemed to be an _____ _____ beside him.'
>
> e   'Neo would never be the kind of wife who went to the lands to _____.'
>
> The second quotation appears to be a direct comment from Head early in the story, explaining to the reader that Neo is unpopular with her family because she looks down on them and boasts about her exam success. However this section is written from the point of view of the disgruntled relatives and so this could be their view of Neo, not the writer's.

Now go back to the story and check all your answers against the details in the story.

Revisiting the text

The next three activities all require close attention to the text.

Get the characters and conflicts covered

The quotations in the quiz should remind you about the three main characters: Neo, Kegoletile and Mathata.

1 Underline the quotations in the text and write some notes on what you think each one shows about the characters and the conflicts they experience.

2 Choose some more brief quotations for Neo, Kegoletile and Mathata. Underline the new quotations and write more notes as before.

Thinking and linking

Look at the following thematic headings:

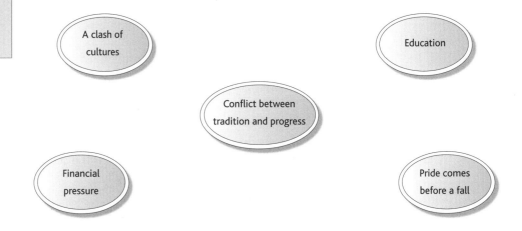

For each of them decide on:
- the moment in the story when you feel Head brings out the theme most strongly
- two other stories in **Opening Worlds** which you feel also bring out this theme.

Looking at language

Focus on the following extract and try to explain as fully as possible how the language Head has chosen brings out some of the story's central ideas. Use the key terms.

> She was a very pretty girl with black eyes like stars; she was always smiling and happy; immediately and always her own natural self. He knew what he was marrying – something quite the opposite, a new kind of girl with false postures and acquired grand-madame ways. And yet, it didn't pay a man these days to look too closely into his heart. **(lines 82–7)**

Key terms

- characterisation
- contrast
- antithesis
- symbolism
- imagery
- simile
- repetition
- listing
- point of view

Nadine Gordimer

OPENING WORLDS

The Train from Rhodesia

Memory joggers

Try the first three activities below without looking at the text.

What happens

Test your memory of what happens in the story by answering the following questions.

1 How many passengers get off the train at the station?

2 Why have the young couple been to Rhodesia?

3 What does the young woman particularly like about the lion carving?

4 How much does the old man want for the carving and how much does the young husband actually pay?

5 Why is the young woman cross with her husband at the end?

Quotation quiz

1 Try to fill in the gaps in these quotations from memory and then decide who says each one, to whom, when, about what and why the quotation is important in the story. The third one has been done for you.

> **a** 'The old man held it up to her still smiling, not from the _____, but at the customer.'
>
> **b** '... the artists sprang, walking bent, like performing _____ ...'
>
> **c** '... the old native, gasping, his <u>skinny</u> toes splaying the sand, flung the lion.'
>
> **d** 'He laughed. I was arguing with him for _____, bargaining – when the train had pulled out already, he came tearing after ...'
>
> **e** 'The black tongue, rolling, like a wave. The mane round the neck. To give one-and-six for that. The heat of _____ mounted through her legs and body ...'
>
> The third quotation is a direct comment from Gordimer which suggests the desperation and poverty of the old man. He is barefoot, old and thin, and is forced to run after the train to secure the cut-price sale. The description helps emphasise the cruel treatment he receives and the contrast between the comfortable world of the train and the poverty of the station.

Now go back to the story and check all your answers against the details in the story.

Character checks and relationships reminders

What memories about the main characters and the development of the story do the following items bring to mind:

- the stationmaster's barefoot children
- faces, behind glass
- the smell of meat cooking with onion?
- vandyke teeth
- chocolates

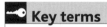
Extension

Imagine you are the young woman at the end of the story. Write your thoughts about the purchase of the lion carving, about your husband and about your future together.

Revisiting the text

The next three activities all require close attention to the text.

Get the characters and conflicts covered

The quotations in the quiz should remind you about the three main characters: the young couple and the old man.

1 Underline the quotations in the text and write some notes on what you think each one shows about the characters, about the ways Gordimer presents them to us and about the conflicts between them.

2 Choose some more brief quotations for the young couple and the old man. Underline the new quotations and write more notes as before.

Thinking and linking

Look at the following thematic headings:

Marital tensions   A clash of cultures   Poverty   Unfairness   Suffering and hardship

For each of them decide on:

- the moment in the story where you feel Gordimer brings out the theme most strongly
- two other stories in **Opening Worlds** which you feel also bring out this theme.

Looking at language

Focus on the following extract and try to explain as fully as possible how the language Gordimer has chosen brings out some of the story's central ideas. Use the key terms.

Key terms

- symbolism
- contrast
- personification
- point of view

A man passed beneath the arch of reaching arms meeting grey-black and white in the exchange of money for the staring wooden eyes, the stiff wooden legs sticking up in the air; went along under the voices and the bargaining, interrogating the wheels. Past the dogs; glancing up at the dining car where he could stare at the faces, behind glass, drinking beer ... (lines 52–7)

Khamsing Srinawk

OPENING WORLDS

The Gold-Legged Frog

Memory joggers

Try the first three activities below without looking at the text.

What happens

Test your memory of what happens in the story by answering the following questions.

1. How many children has Nak Na-ngam?

2. Which child is bitten by the cobra?

3. How is Nak persuaded to leave his son and visit the district office in town?

4. What do his neighbours mean when they describe Nak as 'lucky'?

Quotation quiz

1. Try to fill in the gaps in these quotations from memory and then decide who says each one, to whom, when, about what and why the quotation is important in the story. The first one has been done for you.

---

a 'He recalled the old people had told him this was the <u>portent</u> of drought, want, disaster and death, and he was afraid.'

b 'And then he was shocked almost _____ by the trembling cry of his boy …'

c '"Idiot, don't you have eyes to see people are _____. Get out! Get out and wait outside."'

d 'All you do is _____ if you're born a rice farmer and a subject.'

e '... he strode from the office but had the _____ to say a few words. 'It's noon already. Time for a _____.''

The first quotation is a direct comment from Srinawk showing the reader Nak's troubled thoughts as he returns home exhausted and anxious to be with his poisoned son. Srinawk sets up an ominous feeling of suspense by suggesting that the whirlwind is a sign of bad luck to come and the reference to 'death' hints at the sad ending of the story. He establishes a gloomy mood and the sense of problems piling up for Nak by using alliteration in his list of increasingly serious items: 'drought ... disaster and death'.

Now go back to the story and check all your answers against the details in the story.

Character checks and relationships reminders

What memories about the main characters and the development of the story do the following items bring to mind:

- sunstroke
- the 'last crack'
- the 'fat face' of the deputy district officer?
- the morning meal
- two hundred baht

Extension

Imagine you are Nak waiting for the deputy district officer to return from his lunch. Write your thoughts.

Revisiting the text

The next three activities all require close attention to the text.

Get the characters and conflicts covered

The quotations in the quiz should remind you about the three main characters: Nak, his son and the deputy district officer.

1 Underline the quotations in the text and write some notes on what you think each one shows about the characters, about the ways Srinawk presents them to us and about the conflicts between them.

2 Choose some more brief quotations for Nak, his son and the deputy district officer. Underline the new quotations and write more notes as before.

Thinking and linking

Look at the following thematic headings:

(Poverty)   (Family relationships)   (The cruelty of officials)   (Unfairness (and fate))   (Suffering and hardship)

For each of them decide on:
- the moment in the story when you feel Srinawk brings out the theme most strongly
- two other stories in **Opening Worlds** which you feel also bring out this theme.

Looking at language

Focus on the following extract and try to explain as fully as possible how the language Srinawk has chosen brings out some of the story's central ideas. Use the key terms.

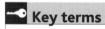
Key terms

- irony
- delay
- suspense
- reversal/twist
- contrast
- pathos
- dialogue

'You sure are lucky.' The words raised his spirits. He smiled a little before repeating expectantly, 'How am I lucky – in what way?'

'The two hundred baht. You got it, didn't you?'

'I got it. It's right here.' He patted his pocket.

'What luck! You sure have good luck, Nak. One more day and you'd been out two hundred baht.' **(lines 137–42)**

Amy Tan
OPENING WORLDS

Two Kinds

Memory joggers

Try the first three activities below without looking at the text.

What happens

Test your memory of what happens in the story by answering the following questions.

1 What has happened to the mother's twin daughters?

2 How old is Jing-mei when her mother begins training her to be a prodigy?

3 How does Jing-mei's mother pay for her piano lessons?

4 Why is old Chong the only one to applaud Jing-mei's public piano performance?

5 What present does Jing-mei receive from her mother on her 30th birthday?

Quotation quiz

1 Try to fill in the gaps in these quotations from memory and then decide who says each one, to whom, when, about what and why the quotation is important in the story. The third one has been done for you.

> **a** 'And after seeing my mother's disappointed face once again, something inside of me began to _____.'
>
> **b** '"Why don't you like me the way I am? I'm not a _____! I can't play the piano. And even if I could, I wouldn't go on TV if you paid me a million dollars!"'
>
> **c** '... her face went blank, her mouth closed, her arms went slack, and she backed out of the room, stunned, as if she were blowing away like a small brown <u>leaf</u>, thin, brittle, lifeless.'
>
> **d** 'For unlike my mother, I did not believe I could be anything I wanted to be. I could only be _____.'
>
> The third quotation comes from Jing-mei, Tan's narrator, when, in the heat of the row about piano lessons, she says that she wishes she were dead like her twin sisters. The description here conveys the mother's shock and the pain of her memories, and the simile comparing her to a fragile autumn leaf suggests the withering of her hopes and dreams for her surviving daughter.

Now go back to the story and check all your answers against the details there.

Character checks and relationships reminders

What memories about the main characters and the development of the story do the following items bring to mind:

- Shirley Temple
- the talent show
- tests
- some old Chinese silk dresses?

Revisiting the text

The next three activities all require close attention to the text.

Get the characters and conflicts covered

The quotations in the quiz should remind you about the two main characters: Jing-mei and her mother.

1 Underline the quotations in the text and write some notes on what you think each one shows about the characters, about the ways Tan presents them to us and about the conflicts between them.

2 Choose some more brief quotations for Jing-mei and her mother. Underline the quotations and write more notes as before.

Thinking and linking

Look at the following thematic headings:

 Family relationships

A clash of cultures

 Poverty

Unfairness

 Achievement or disappointment

For each of them decide on:
- the moment in the story when you feel Tan brings out the theme most strongly
- two other stories in **Opening Worlds** which you feel also bring out this theme.

Looking at language

Focus on the following extract and try to explain as fully as possible how the language Tan has chosen brings out some of the story's central ideas. Use the key terms.

'You want me to be someone that I'm not!' I sobbed. 'I'll never be the kind of daughter you want me to be!'

'Only two kinds of daughters,' she shouted in Chinese. 'Those who are obedient and those who follow their own mind! Only one kind of daughter can live in this house. Obedient daughter!'

'Then I wish I wasn't your daughter. I wish you weren't my mother,' I shouted. As I said these things I got scared. It felt like worms and toads and slimy things crawling out of my chest, but it also felt good, as if this awful side of me had surfaced at last.' **(lines 330–8)**

🔑 Key terms

- contrast
- point of view
- narrator
- persona
- characterisation
- climax
- dialogue
- simile

Feng Ji-Cai

OPENING WORLDS

The Tall Woman and her Short Husband

Memory joggers

Try the first three activities below without looking at the text.

What happens

Test your memory of what happens in the story by answering the following questions.

1. Who is the main persecutor of Mrs Tall and Mr Short?

2. What happy event occurs after three years of marriage?

3. What is Mr Short's well-paid job?

4. What crime is he accused of in 1966?

5. How long does he spend in prison?

6. Why does the tailor's wife visit him at the end of the story?

Quotation quiz

1. Try to fill in the gaps in these quotations from memory and then decide who says each one, to whom, when, about what and why the quotation is important in the story. The third one has been done for you.

a 'She seemed dried up and scrawny with a face like an unvarnished _____.'

b 'Her husband on the other hand seemed a rubber _____ ...'

c 'They must have something to <u>hide</u>, those two. Why else should they keep to themselves?'

d 'In that period of _____ people took leave of their senses and cruelly made up groundless accusations in order to find some Hitler in their midst.'

e 'As she couldn't raise her left foot, he tied a rope around it and pulled this up when she wanted to take a step forward. This was a pathetic yet _____ sight, and the neighbours were touched by it.'

The third quotation is taken from early in the story and is a piece of the tailor's wife's dialogue expressing her view of the married couple to the residents of Unity Mansions. It demonstrates her nosiness and her suspicion of what she sees as unusual behaviour. She encourages her neighbours to share her suspicions and her question does create suspense and curiosity for the reader. As the story develops, we see the irony that although she prides herself on her understanding of the couple she is always wrong about them. What's 'hidden' from her here, ironically, is the simple fact that they love each other and just want to be together.

Extension

In lines 206–8, we are told: 'Mrs Tall neither nodded nor shook her head. She had seen through the tailor's wife too. Her eyes glinted with derision and contempt.' Imagine that you are Mrs Tall at this point in the story. Write your thoughts.

Now go back to the story and check all your answers against the details in the story.

Character checks and relationships reminders

What memories about the main characters and the development of the story do the following items bring to mind:

- Unity Mansions
- the small gatehouse
- the sound of breaking glass
- the umbrella?

Revisiting the text

The next three activities all require close attention to the text.

Get the characters and conflicts covered

The quotations in the quiz should remind you about the three main characters: Mrs Tall, Mr Short and the tailor's wife.

1 Underline the quotations in the text and write some notes on what you think each one shows about the characters, about the ways Ji-Cai presents them to us and about the conflicts between them.

2 Choose more brief quotations for Mrs Tall, Mr Short and the tailor's wife. Underline the new quotations and write more notes as before.

Thinking and linking

Look at the following thematic headings:

Love   Prejudice   Courage   Unfairness   Suffering and hardship

Key terms

- narrator
- point of view
- contrast
- characterisation
- colloquial language
- rhetorical question
- imperative
- second-person pronoun
- present tense
- characterisation
- simile
- metaphor

For each of them decide on:

- the moment in the story where you feel Ji-Cai brings out the theme most strongly
- two other stories in **Opening Worlds** which you feel also bring out this theme.

Looking at language

Focus on the following extract and try to explain as fully as possible how the language Ji-Cai has chosen brings out some of the story's central ideas. Use the key terms.

Or again, would you choose a wife ten years older than you, heftier than you or a head taller than you? Don't be in a rush to answer. Here's an instance of such a couple.

She was seventeen centimetres taller than he. One point seven five metres in height, she towered above most of her sex like a crane over chickens. (lines 16–21)

Karl Sealy

OPENING WORLDS

The Pieces of Silver

Memory joggers

Try the first three activities below without looking at the text.

What happens

Test your memory of what happens in the story by answering the following questions.

1. What happens to boys who contribute a shilling to the Head's leaving present?

2. What happens to boys who contribute nothing?

3. Who gives Clement the idea of raising money by singing?

4. Their last visit is to the house of a Mr Megahey who gives them their 'biggest taking of the night ... sixpence'. What is ironic about this?

Character checks and relationships reminders

What memories about the main characters and the development of the story do the following items bring to mind:

- the cane of plaited tamarind stalks
- chalk
- Julius Caesar
- paper and comb
- eight pieces of silver?

Quotation quiz

1. Try to fill in the gaps in these quotations from memory and then decide who says each one, to whom, when, about what and why the quotation is important in the story. The last one has been done for you.

> a 'The acting Head was a squat _____ of a man, fierce-eyed and unsmiling.'
>
> b 'The house was a poor, wretched _____ of a room ...'
>
> c 'Her plate was resting on her lap, and she scraped and pecked and foraged her food like a _____ _____ ...'
>
> d 'She listened as attentively as a _____, and as she listened, she put her hand around his neck and drew his head gently down upon her young bosom.'
>
> e '"There are eight," he told the gaping schoolmaster. "One for each of us."'
>
> f 'His voice struck through the silent school, clear and thrilling as a star's light.'

The last quotation is taken from the end of the story and contains a line of Clement's dialogue addressed to Mr Chase, the acting Head, and a line of description from Sealy describing Clement's moment of triumph. It is a satisfying ending because Clement turns the tables on Chase, depriving him of the 'enjoyment' of humiliating the boys again. He also teaches Chase a lesson about generosity and leaves him 'gaping' with shock by providing a contribution for seven other boys. The scene is set on the assembly platform and Clement's victory over Chase contrasts with the shame he felt during assembly on the previous day. Sealy's simile describing the quality and effect of Clement's voice as 'clear and thrilling as a star's light' suggests his pride and triumph, and the metaphor 'struck' personifies the powerful impact of Clement's dramatic final announcement.

Now go back to the story and check all your answers against the details there.

Extension

In line 232, Evelina says to Clement, "'Now I going tell you how we'll fix that brute, Mr Chase.'" Write the conversation between Evelina and Clement.

Revisiting the text

The next three activities all require close attention to the text.

Get the characters and conflicts covered

The quotations in the quiz should remind you about the main characters: Clement, Evelina, their parents and Chase.

1 Underline the quotations in the text and write some notes on what you think each one shows about the characters, about the ways Sealy presents them to us and about the conflicts between them.

2 Choose more brief quotations for Clement, Evelina, their parents and Chase. Underline the new quotations and write more notes as before.

Thinking and linking

Look at the following thematic headings:

Poverty
Family relationships
The cruelty of officials
Unfairness
Suffering and hardship

Key terms

- dialogue
- irony
- contrast
- characterisation
- dialect/non-standard English
- rhetorical questions

For each of them decide on:
- the moment when you feel Sealy brings out the theme most strongly
- two other stories in **Opening Worlds** which you feel also bring out this theme.

Looking at language

Focus on the following extract. Explain as fully as possible how the language Sealy has chosen brings out some of the story's central ideas. Use the key terms.

'Hmn. Wa' threepence boy? Why in de name of de Lord must poor starving people got to find threepences for Jim Megahey what's got his belly sitting so pretty wi' fat?' (lines 140–2)

Ismith Khan

OPENING WORLDS

The Red Ball

Memory joggers

Try the first three activities below without looking at the text.

What happens

Test your memory of what happens in the story by answering the following questions.

1. How long have Bolan and his family been in Port of Spain?

2. Why does Bolan visit Woodford Square each evening?

3. Why does he steal from his parents?

4. What happens in Bolan's 'dream' and how do you explain it?

Character checks and relationships reminders

What memories about the main characters and the development of the story do the following items bring to mind:

- the names that the other boys call Bolan
- black pudding
- the father's hair and beard
- switches of sawn-off wood?

- Bolan's bowling
- Black Cat rum
- the Capstan tin

Quotation quiz

1. Try to remember these quotations and then decide who says each one, to whom, when, about what and why the quotation is important in the story.

> a   "'Leave the child alone!'"
>
> b   'The boy's eyelid jerked up and his eyes met his mother's and he saw her look back quickly into the brazier.'
>
> c   "'What come over you at all? The child have a name ...'"
>
> d   "'One day when we pay back everybody we will be able to save something ...'"
>
> e   'For each moment of defence from his mother, the boy got more stinging lashes on his legs.'
>
> f   'When she saw the ball, she knew that they had finally asked him to play.'

Now go back to the story and check all your answers against the details in the story.

Revisiting the text

The next three activities all require close attention to the text.

Get the characters and conflicts covered

You have probably noticed that the six quotations in the quiz above all relate to Bolan's mother. There are four extracts from her dialogue and two examples of Ismith Khan describing her thoughts or actions.

1 Underline the six quotations in the text and write some notes on what you think each one shows about the family conflicts, about Bolan's mother as a character and about the way Khan presents her to us. For the first quotation, for example:

'Leave the child alone!'

- dialogue
- defends son strongly
- stands up to husband and stops him from taking out his frustrations on Bolan
- loving and protective mother
- knows Bolan is unhappy in the city
- contrast with father.

2 Choose six brief quotations each for Bolan and his father. Underline the quotations and add your own notes as before.

Thinking and linking

Look at the following thematic headings:

Poverty and hardship   Feeling left out   Adjusting to new situations   Parents and children (love and conflict)

For each of them decide on:
- the moment in the story where you feel Khan brings out the theme most strongly
- two other stories in **Opening Worlds** which you feel also bring out this theme.

Looking at language

Focus on the following extract and try to explain as fully as possible how the language Khan has chosen brings out some of the story's central ideas. Use the key terms.

'He had touched the strong green veins running down the calves of the man's legs with fear, half expecting the severe lips to smile, or even curl in anger at him, but the lips stood still in their severity.' (lines 19–22)

Ruth Prawer Jhabvala

The Young Couple

Memory joggers

Try the first three activities below without looking at the text.

What happens

Test your memory of what happens in the story by answering the following questions.

1. Who pays for Cathy and Naraian's living expenses and for their flat?

2. When are Cathy and Naraian at their happiest?

3. Why doesn't Cathy get a job?

4. Why does Cathy visit the city bazaar on her own?

5. What prompts Naraian to accept a job with his uncle?

6. Where are Cathy and Naraian going to live at the end of the story?

Quotation quiz

1. Try to fill in the gaps in these quotations from memory and then decide who says each one, to whom, when, about what and why the quotation is important in the story. The first one has been done for you.

> **a** '... all their English friends envied them because of the challenge, the life of <u>purpose</u>, that awaited them.'
>
> **b** 'But here, when they were in public places, Naraian took care to see that there was a _____ few inches of space always between them ...'
>
> **c** 'She met plenty of people but they were all Naraian's friends or his family, so that she began to feel almost as if they were forming a _____ round her out of which she could not break.'
>
> **d** '"Our girls don't go into these bazaars alone. It is not _____ for us."'
>
> The first quotation is a direct comment from Jhabvala showing that the new life awaiting Cathy and Naraian in India appears exciting and worthy at first, especially from the point of view of their English friends. There is irony in the way that, in reality, there is no idealism and sense of purpose in the life the young couple lead in India, as they become increasingly bored, restless and dependent on Naraian's family.

Now go back to the story and check all your answers against the details in the story.

Character checks and relationships reminders

What memories about the main characters and the development of the story do the following items bring to mind:

- the sweeper-woman
- Sunday lunches
- Naraian's friends
- the eating of a mango?

Extension

Imagine that you are a friend of Cathy's who is able to talk to her about her decision to move to India with Naraian at the start of the story. What advice about adapting to life in her new country would you give her?

Revisiting the text

The next three activities all require close attention to the text.

Get the characters and conflicts covered

The quotations in the quiz should remind you about the three main characters: Cathy, Naraian and Naraian's parents.

1 Underline the quotations in the text and write some notes on what you think each one shows about the characters, about the ways Naraian presents them to us and about the conflicts between them.

2 Choose some more brief quotations which reveal details about Cathy, Naraian and Naraian's parents. Underline the new quotations and write more notes as before.

Thinking and linking

Look at the following thematic headings:

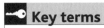

Family relationships   A culture clash   Love   Power   Money

For each of them decide on:

- the moment in the story where you feel Jhabvala brings out the theme most strongly
- two other stories in **Opening Worlds** which you feel also bring out this theme.

Looking at language

Key terms

- irony
- reversal/twist
- contrast
- point of view
- imagery
- symbolism
- repetition
- characterisation

Focus on the following extract and try to explain as fully as possible how the language Jhabvala has chosen brings out some of the story's central ideas. Use the key terms.

They kissed. The kiss was delicious but, even while it was going on and set within it as in a heartshaped frame, she had a vision of the room that was being got ready for them: the same heavy, shiny furniture as the rest of the house, a carpet, ample satin bedspreads matching the curtains. (lines 498–502)

R. K. Narayan

OPENING WORLDS

Leela's Friend

Memory joggers

Try the first three activities below without looking at the text.

What happens

Test your memory of what happens in the story by answering the following questions.

1. How old is Leela?

2. What is Sidda's most important job as the Sivasankers' servant?

3. Where does Sidda sit and where does he sleep?

4. What does Sidda do when Mrs Sivasanker threatens him with the police?

5. How do the Sivasankers react to the proof of Sidda's innocence?

Quotation quiz

1. Try to fill in the gaps in these quotations from memory and then decide who says each one, to whom, when, about what and why the quotation is important in the story. The first one has been done for you.

---

a '... it looked as though Leela would keep him there pinned to his seat until his stiff, inflexible wrist <u>cracked</u>.'

b '"Why should not Sidda sit in our _____, Mother?' Mother didn't answer the question.

c '"He has taken away your gold chain.'"
   "_____ _____. I will have a new chain,' Leela said."

d '"I have not taken it,' Sidda said feebly, looking at the _____."

e 'She clung to Sidda's hand. He looked at her mutely, like an _____.'

The first quotation is a direct comment from R. K. Narayan showing Sidda's patient devotion to Leela. He endures the humiliation and physical discomfort of the school game and allows Leela to boss him about without a word of complaint. Narayan's characterisation of him here as noble and long-suffering makes the later treatment of him appear even more cruel and unfair.

Now go back to the story and check all your answers against the details in the story.

Character checks and relationships reminders

What memories about the main characters and the development of the story do the following items bring to mind:

- the moon
- 'school hour'
- the gold chain
- the tamarind pot?

Extension

Look carefully at the way Mr and Mrs Sivasanker handle their daughter throughout the story. What advice would you like to give them about bringing up children?

Revisiting the text

The next three activities all require close attention to the text.

Get the characters and conflicts covered

The quotations in the quiz should remind you about the main characters: Sidda, Leela and Leela's parents.

1 Underline the quotations in the text and write some notes on what you think each one shows about the characters, about the ways Narayan presents them to us and about the conflicts between them.

2 Choose some more brief quotations for Sidda, Leela and Leela's parents. Underline the new quotations and write more notes as before.

Thinking and linking

Look at the following thematic headings:

Family relationships   Prejudice   Poverty (and class divisions)   Unfairness   The cruelty of officials

For each of them decide on:

- the moment in the story where you feel Narayan brings out the theme most strongly
- two other stories in **Opening Worlds** which you feel also bring out this theme.

Looking at language

Focus on the following extract and try to explain as fully as possible how the language Narayan has chosen brings out some of the story's central ideas. Use the key words.

She shuddered to think what a villain she had been harboring all these days. It was God's mercy that he hadn't killed the girl for the chain ... 'Sleep, Leela, sleep,' she cajoled.

'Can't you tell the story of the elephant?' Leela asked.

'No.' (lines 112–7)

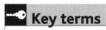
Key terms

- irony
- reversal/twist
- contrast
- point of view
- characterisation
- hyperbole
- dialogue

Anita Desai

OPENING WORLDS

Games at Twilight

Memory joggers

Try the first three activities below without looking at the text.

What happens

Test your memory of what happens in the story by answering the following questions.

1. How many of the children can you name?

2. Who seem to be the oldest and the youngest boys?

3. Why can't Ravi hide in the garage?

4. Why does he want to win the game so badly?

5. Why is he so upset at the end of the story?

Quotation quiz

1. Try to fill in the gaps in these quotations from memory and then decide who says each one, to whom, when, about what and why the quotation is important in the story. The second one has been done for you.

> a '... she actually let down the bolt of the front door so that they burst out like _____ from a cracking, over-ripe pod ...'
>
> b 'He hugged his knees together and smiled to himself almost shyly at the thought of so much victory, such <u>laurels</u>.'
>
> c '"The grass is green,
>   The rose is red;
>   Remember me
>   When I am _____ ..."'
>
> d 'He lay down full length on the damp grass, crushing his face into it, no longer crying, silenced by a terrible sense of his _____.'
>
> The second quotation is a direct comment from Desai showing the reader, from Ravi's point of view, how much he wants to win the game. He is sitting in the shed imagining the triumph of beating older children and of having his achievement recognised – like a champion who is crowned with laurels. Desai is setting up the crushing irony of the ending where Ravi receives no recognition whatsoever.

Now go back to the story and check all your answers against the details in the story.

Character checks and relationships reminders

What memories about the main characters and the development of the story do the following items bring to mind:

- Raghu's legs
- the shed
- the spider
- the chant?

Revisiting the text

The next three activities all require close attention to the text.

Get the characters and conflicts covered

The quotations in the quiz should remind you about the main characters: Ravi, his mother and the other children.

1 Underline the quotations in the text and write some notes on what you think each one shows about the characters, about the ways Desai presents them to us and about the conflicts between them.

2 Choose some more brief quotations for Ravi, his mother and the other children.

3 Underline the new quotations and write more notes as before.

Thinking and linking

Look at the following thematic headings:

Family relationships   Death   Feeling left out   Growing up   Achievement or disappointment

For each of them decide on:

- the moment in the story where you feel Desai brings out the theme most strongly
- two other stories in **Opening Worlds** which you feel also bring out this theme.

Looking at language

Focus on the following extract and try to explain as fully as possible how the language Desai has chosen brings out some of the story's central ideas. Use the key terms.

And the arc of thin arms trembled in the twilight, and the heads were bowed so sadly, and their feet tramped to that melancholy refrain so mournfully, so helplessly, that Ravi could not bear it. He would not follow them, he would not be included in this funereal game. He had wanted victory and triumph – not a funeral. **(lines 256–60)**

Yuri Nagibin

OPENING WORLDS

The Winter Oak

Memory joggers

Try the first three activities below without looking at the text.

What happens

Test your memory of what happens in the story by answering the following questions.

1. How long has Anna Vasilevna been a teacher?

2. Why is Anna so worried about Savushkin that she arranges to meet his mother?

3. Why doesn't this meeting take place?

4. What does Anna think is 'the most amazing thing in the forest' at the end of the story?

Character checks and relationships reminders

What memories about the main characters and the development of the story do the following items bring to mind:

- Savushkin's boots
- an elk
- parts of speech
- warm springs?

Quotation quiz

1. Try to fill in the gaps in these quotations from memory and then decide who says each one, to whom, when, about what and why the quotation is important in the story. The first one has been done for you.

> a 'And she remembered too how she used to be tormented by a <u>ridiculous</u> fear that perhaps they would not understand her.'
>
> b 'The words were torn out of his soul, like a confession, or a _____ secret which he could not keep from spilling out of his heart.'
>
> c 'As soon as they stepped into the forest and the fir branches that looked like paws heavily laden with snow closed behind them, they were immediately transported into another world, an _____ world of peace and silence.'
>
> d 'In the middle of the glade, clothed in glittering white raiment, huge and majestic as a _____, stood an oak.'
>
> e 'Savushkin blushed; he very much wanted to say to the schoolmistress that he would never be late again, but he was afraid of telling a _____.'

The first quotation is a direct comment from Nagibin showing the reader Anna's point of view and thoughts. The comment, and the word 'ridiculous' in particular, are intended to be ironic because, as the rest of the story demonstrates, Anna and her pupils inhabit different worlds. It is only at the end of the story that Anna begins to understand what is important to her pupils and to see her lessons on parts of speech as dry and inadequate.

Now go back to the story and check all your answers against the details in the story.

Revisiting the text

The next three activities all require close attention to the text.

Get the characters and conflicts covered

The quotations in the quiz should remind you about the three main characters: Anna, Savushkin – and you could include the winter oak itself, as it is described as a person (personified) so often.

1 Underline the quotations in the text and write some notes on what you think each one shows about the characters, about the ways Narayan presents them to us and about the conflicts between them.

2 Choose some more brief quotations for Anna, Savushkin and the winter oak. Underline the new quotations and write more notes as before.

Thinking and linking

Look at the following thematic headings:

Prejudice   Poverty   Education   Unfairness   The cruelty of officials   A culture clash

For each of them decide on:
- the moment in the story where you feel Nagibin brings out the theme most strongly
- two other stories in **Opening Worlds** which you feel also bring out this theme.

Looking at language

Focus on the following extract and try to explain as fully as possible how the language Nagibin has chosen brings out some of the story's central ideas. Use the key terms.

'Today we are going to continue learning about parts of speech.'

The class quietened down, and a heavy lorry with a trailer could be heard crawling along the road. **(lines 8–10)**

◎ **Extension**

In the story, it is possible that Savushkin, the pupil, has learned one lesson – that 'oak' is a noun. Anna, the teacher, on the other hand, learns many lessons – about the natural world, Savushkin and herself. List the five most important lessons she learns.

🔑 **Key terms**

- irony
- contrast
- point of view
- characterisation
- symbolism
- personification
- dialogue

OPENING WORLDS

English Lit Unit 2
- 45 mins to answer
- Choice of 3 questions
- Worth 25% of mark

Tackling the question

> Explore the ways in which the writers of *two* stories in this collection make you feel sympathy for a parent. Remember to support your answer with detail from each story.

 1 Choosing your question

As you skim the story titles (six for English and all twelve for English Literature) on the Contents page of **Opening Worlds**, ask yourself:
- do parents spring to mind
- does my story concept map (see page 80) include 'parents and children'
- am I sure what 'sympathy' means
- do my favourite or best-prepared stories feature sympathetic parents
- have I tackled a similar question as part of my revision?

If you keep answering 'no', don't choose this question. If you keep answering 'yes' to most of the above, go on to choose your stories.

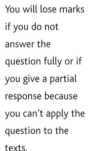

! Remember

You will lose marks if you do not answer the question fully or if you give a partial response because you can't apply the question to the texts.

 2 Choosing your stories and characters

To find the best stories for you to answer the question, ask yourself:
- how many stories mention parents
- of those nine, how many stories feature parents
- of those six, how many stories feature parents who are sympathetic
- of those four, how many stories present the parent and his/her relationship with his/her child fully enough for me to build up a solid answer?

So, you might narrow it down to the following three choices:
- ✔ the father in **The Gold-Legged Frog**
- ✔ the mother in **Two Kinds**
- ✔ the mother or the father in **The Red Ball**.

Finally, choose the two characters and two stories which have made the strongest impression on you.

💡 Top tip

Use your plan to keep your answer on track.

 3 Planning your answer

You need to make a quick outline plan to help you structure your ideas.

a Underline the key words in the question.

> Explore the <u>ways</u> in which the writers of *two* stories in this collection make you feel <u>sympathy</u> for a <u>parent</u>. Remember to support your answer with <u>detail</u> from each story.

Decide what the key words mean and think about what you are being asked to comment on:

- the ways – the writers' methods
- parent – the character as a parent
- sympathy – pity, understanding, respect, admiration, empathy
- detail – references to the stories, quotations.

! Remember

Planning helps you think up and sort out your ideas and improves the structure and focus of your essays.

🔆 Top tip

It can help to put the question to yourself in different ways, for example:
- how do the writers make me feel sorry for these two parents?
- what is there in the presentation of these two parents and their situations which makes me share their feelings?

b Brainstorm ideas and make a few notes for each of your two parents. Jot down some reminders about textual details and quotations you could use to support these points. The following example is on **The Red Ball**:

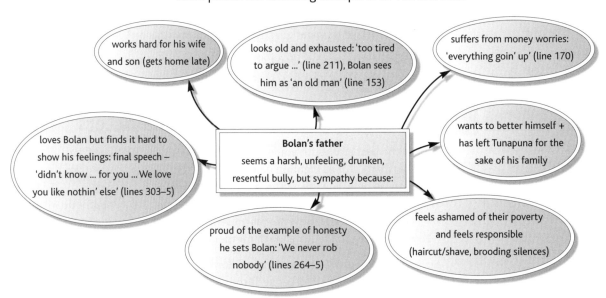

works hard for his wife and son (gets home late)

looks old and exhausted: 'too tired to argue ...' (line 211), Bolan sees him as 'an old man' (line 153)

suffers from money worries: 'everything goin' up' (line 170)

loves Bolan but finds it hard to show his feelings: final speech – 'didn't know ... for you ... We love you like nothin' else' (lines 303–5)

Bolan's father
seems a harsh, unfeeling, drunken, resentful bully, but sympathy because:

wants to better himself + has left Tunapuna for the sake of his family

proud of the example of honesty he sets Bolan: 'We never rob nobody' (lines 264–5)

feels ashamed of their poverty and feels responsible (haircut/shave, brooding silences)

Do a similar planning brainstorm for Nak in **The Gold-Legged Frog**.

c Working from the brainstorms, decide how you would order the points. Give each point a number according to the order in which you would write about them. Discuss and compare your ideas with a partner.

! Remember

An introduction shows the examiner your overall approach and guides them into what you think about the stories.

4 Writing your answer

a **Opening paragraph**
Write your opening paragraph, using the following guidelines. First, introduce both of your chosen parents and their situations. Then in one or two sentences suggest general reasons for sympathy, although not in any detail yet, but using the key words from the question.

Top tip

Keep introductions brief and clear; leave the detail to the main part of your answer.

b **Following paragraphs**

Use the guidelines given on page 114 to write the main part of your answer. Remember to start each new paragraph with a point which clearly relates to the question, for example:

> 'Srinawk encourages sympathy for Nak by emphasising his physical exhaustion and concern for 'his little son' at the start of the story ...'

Also use the three-point formula:

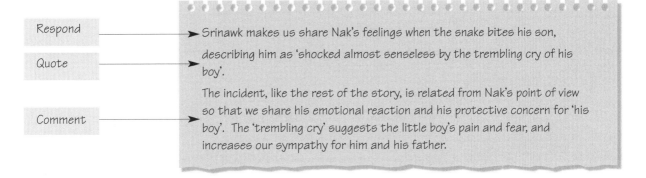

Respond → Srinawk makes us share Nak's feelings when the snake bites his son,

Quote → describing him as 'shocked almost senseless by the trembling cry of his boy'.

Comment → The incident, like the rest of the story, is related from Nak's point of view so that we share his emotional reaction and his protective concern for 'his boy'. The 'trembling cry' suggests the little boy's pain and fear, and increases our sympathy for him and his father.

c **Final paragraph**

Your conclusion should refer to both characters: you could suggest which of the characters you find more sympathetic. Also try to offer a fresh perspective so you are not just repeating yourself, for example you could look at the effect of the two endings – both ironic twists and both crushingly sad.

 5 Checking your answer

Errors cost marks so take the time to check your written expression and the spelling of all names. Correct any other slips of the pens and add any after thoughts showing clearly where they go.

Looking at candidates' answers

All the candidates below make good, relevant points but only one makes full use of the three-point formula. Find that one candidate and explain where the others fall short.

> Teresa
>
> I feel sympathy for Nak because he is a very poor man.

Top tips

- If your 'comments' aren't the longest parts of your paragraphs, spend more time developing your ideas.
- Focus your 'comment' on details such as one or two words from your quotation. Broaden out your comments from there.

Josh

I feel sympathy for Nak because he is so poor that he and his children have to search for frogs for their breakfast.

Ravi

Srinawk increases my sympathy for Nak by emphasising his poverty and the cruel treatment he receives from the officials. He is anxious to return to his dying son but needs the 'two hundred baht' and they make him wait while they take their lunch break. Srinawk reveals Nak's dejected thoughts ('All you do is suffer if you're born a rice farmer and a subject') to make the reader share his misery and helplessness.

Clinton

I feel sympathy for Nak because he is so poor. 'We're awful poor' he says to the official.

Debra

I feel sympathy for Nak because his poverty puts him at the mercy of uncaring officials. 'All you do is suffer if you're born a rice farmer and a subject,' he says.

The star of the three-point formula is Ravi, who shows awareness of the writer and of the question as well as commenting fully on the effect of the brief quotations he has selected. If he continues to work at this level across the whole course, he could get an A* overall.

What are the strengths and weaknesses of the following paragraphs taken from two different candidates' answers to Question 1? Who is likely to get a higher mark? You can try to grade them if you like!

Louise

Although Bolans father drinks, lets 'his hair grow' and looks 'like an old man', I feel sympathy for him because of the way that he still pretends to people back in Tunapuna that life is alot better than it really is in Port of Spain. A sense of sympathy is created not only because he works hard for his family and for very little money, but also because he is unable to admit to the people back in Tunapuna that life in the big city isn't all that he was hoping for.

> Ben
>
> We are made to feel sypathy towards the farther because of how hard he works and yet how poor they all are 'The man for the room rent come and he say that next week price goin up by two shillings,' she said as if she were speaking to herself. 'It look as if every thing goin up since we come to live in town is always the same damn thing, as soon as you have a shilling save … two shillings expense come out' this makes us feel sypathy because he can barly afford this one room place.

Examiner's comments

<u>General features to reward:</u> Both answers make use of the text, selecting relevant detail and quoting from it directly. Both answers show awareness of the question's focus on sympathy and display some personal response to the plight of the family. Both answers make a case for sympathising with Bolan's father which is not a simple or obvious approach to this story or this question. The two candidates see that he's more than just a drunken bully.

<u>Louise</u> is very skilful at selecting brief quotations from the text and fitting them neatly into her sentences (lets 'his hair grow' … looks 'like an old man') and she constructs nicely argumentative sentences ('Although' – you know a contradiction is coming; 'not only because' – you know an additional point is coming). She states a clear personal response directly ('I feel sympathy') and then gives reasons supporting this response. However the answer is slightly repetitive (there is no real need to mention the people back in Tunapuna twice), doesn't always support ideas with evidence (how do we know that Bolan's father works hard for very little money?) and doesn't look closely at the writing. There's a slight anxiety about relevance in that Louise seems to be answering a slightly different question (on general sympathy for Bolan's father) as if she's tackled this before in class, rather than really engaging the central idea of him as a parent. There are also a couple of slips in accuracy ('Bolans father' and 'alot' as one word). Nevertheless, if Louise keeps up writing of this quality throughout her exams and coursework, it should bring her a comfortable Grade B overall.

<u>Ben</u> uses textual evidence of the family's hardship ('the one room place … ') and makes a case for sympathy, although like Louise, he doesn't demonstrate how we know that Bolan's father works hard, and he seems to be tackling a question about general sympathy for Bolan's father rather than looking at his relationship with Bolan and engaging the wording of this question directly. He uses a quotation which is unnecessarily long and which is not closely related to the point he is making, and then tacks on a comment about 'sympathy' which tends to repeat a previous point, rather than going on to explore the significance of the quotation or to comment on the effect of the language. He also finds it difficult to fit the long quotation neatly into his paragraph and so just drops it in without so much as an introductory colon or an indication of who exactly is speaking. Ben's expression falters on several occasions ('sypathy', 'farther', 'barly', some slips in copying out the long quotation and some unclear sentence boundaries). Work of this quality should bring Ben a Grade D overall.

Complete sample answer

Read the following full answer to this question and decide whether you agree with the examiner's comments and with the final mark out of 20.

Good opening. Engages question and both stories. Focuses on writers.

Tariq

Khamsing Srinawks central character, Nak, suffers a great deal in 'The Gold-Legged Frog' and is easier to feel sorry for than Bolan's father in 'The Red Ball'. Nevertheless Ismith Khan uses a variety of ways to make the reader feel sorry for Bolan's father who although an uncaring, violent father at first glance, upon further dissection reveals a more pathetic, helpless, loving father.

Personal response. Good.

My first impressions of Bolan's father are unpleasant especially where his jealousy of his son comes into play and he tries to correct his speech, saying 'you beginning to play big shot.' This clearly shows the feeling of inadequacy that Bolan's father bares because his son is getting an education and his later beating of Bolan is very violent.

Seeing different interpretation. Good.

However Ismith Khan does evoke feelings of sympathy for the father. He never had the opportunities that Bolan has as they weren't offered to him – 'you don't know how lucky you is to be going to school, when I was your age ... ' This shows that the father values his son's education and doesn't want him to take it for granted.

Packed with references to the text.

I also feel sorry for him because he feels that he is to blame for the unhappiness of the family as it was his decision to leave Tunapuna. His silences, his drinking and his temper are all because of his feelings of guilt. He tries to keep up appearances when he goes back to Tunapuna and doesn't want Bolan to hear 'big people talk' about their money worries.

Excellent three-point formula. Fits brief quotations into his sentences. Comments on effect.

Ismith Khans description of him shows that he is exhausted by all his hard work and money worries. Bolan notices that he looks 'like an old man', lets 'his hair grow', makes 'a terrible grimace' before speaking and sighs with 'relief and tiredness' when he lies down. I find it very sad that Bolan sees these changes in his father.

Excellent linking as he moves from one story to the next.

Nak in 'The Gold-Legged Frog' is even poorer than Bolan's father and he also has to cope with a life and death situation for his son so it's very easy to feel sympathy for him. Also, like Bolan's father, Srinawk shows us that he blames himself for what happens to his son. He thinks back to the snake-bite and wishes that he'd done things differently – 'If only he had gone home then, the poor child would be all right now' – and the reader shares his thoughts and feelings. His reaction to the snake-bite is described in a dramatic way ('he was shocked almost senseless') to show his strong feelings for his son. He obviously loves the 'poor child' who is often called 'his little son' or 'his boy' to show how close they are.

Strong sense of writer's methods – creating sympathy. Excellent selection and use of brief quotations.

Excellent cluster of references to the text.	Srinawk shows us Nak suffering in other ways as well. He suffers from sunstroke and blistered feet and a whirlwind as if even the weather is against him. The deputy district officer treats him cruelly, making him wait even though he's worried about his son. Nak's thoughts sum up his despair – 'All you do is suffer if you're born a rice farmer and a subject' – as if he has no control of what happens and this gives me sympathy for his helplessness.
Excellent three-point formula. Response, quotation, comment – in one sentence.	Both writers end their stories with a twist which makes the reader feel sorry for both fathers. Bolan's father's final words show he does care for his son and he says he's working for him alone. His inability to tell Bolan while he is awake is used by the writer to evoke sympathy. The twist for Nak is very cruel because when the neighbours call him 'lucky' they raise his hopes for his son, but they are talking about the 'two hundred baht' which he didn't even want to get – and it means that his son is dead.
Polished conclusion. Links the endings and the fathers. Strong argument for sympathy emerges.	

Examiner's comment

Well planned answer. Knows both stories well and makes fine use of textual detail and brief, well-focused quotations. Really concentrates on the wording of the question and shapes a relevant, personal case for sympathy. Tries to show awareness of the writers and to discuss their choices and techniques (the physical descriptions, the sharing of the character's thoughts, the use of Bolan's point-of-view, the final twists ...) rather than just describing the characters and their sad situations. Clearly and accurately expressed.

Would you give Tariq the full marks – a top A*? It's easy to pick out a few possible weaknesses, in fact. Tariq spends more time on Bolan's father, as if he's more confident about that story and he doesn't always sustain 'a strong awareness of the writers at work' as the Band 1 descriptor says. He spells 'bears' as 'bares', he misses out a few possessive apostrophes ('Srinawk's', 'Khan's' ...), doesn't always fit quotations neatly into his sentences and some of the expression (as in the final sentence) is not fluent. However, an examiner's job is to reward and there is so much to reward here. A top mark does not mean that the answer is perfect or includes every possible point. It means an excellent effort for a 16-year-old in 45 minutes under exam conditions – and that's what Tariq manages here.

- English Lit Unit 2
- 45 mins to answer
- Choice of 3 questions
- Worth 25% of mark

Tackling the question

> Choose *two* stories from **Opening Worlds** which you find both moving and amusing. How do the writers of each story arouse these responses in you? Remember to support your ideas with details from the texts.

1 Choosing your question

As you skim the story titles (six for English and all twelve for English Literature) on the Contents page of **Opening Worlds**, ask yourself:

- have I found funny elements in some of the stories, even if they deal with serious and emotional issues
- am I able to explain how the writing amuses me rather than just picking out 'funny bits'
- does my story concept map (see page 80) include 'humour' or a similar theme
- have I tackled a similar question as part of my revision?

If you keep answering 'no', don't choose this question. If you keep answering 'yes' to most of the above, go on to choose your stories.

! Remember

You will lose marks if you do not answer the question fully or if you give a partial response because you can't apply the question to the texts.

2 Choosing your stories

To find the best stories for you to answer the question, ask yourself:
- how many of the stories could I describe as 'moving'
- of these, how many of the stories have amusing moments
- of these nine, how many of these stories use humour fully enough for me to build up a solid answer?

So, you might narrow it down to the following three choices:
- ✔ **Two Kinds**
- ✔ **The Tall Woman and Her Short Husband**
- ✔ **The Pieces of Silver**.

It's possible that you have come up with a completely different shortlist here. Different people find different things amusing. Examiners will be happy with other choices as long as you can support your arguments with attention to the writing. For example, you could shape good arguments about the amusing humiliation of arrogant characters in **Dead Men's Path** and **Snapshots of a Wedding**, or point out the amusing ironies of children showing up their elders and 'betters' in **Leela's Friend** and **The Winter Oak**. However the three listed stories probably provide the most clear-cut examples.

3 Planning your answer

You need to make a quick outline plan to help you structure your ideas.

a Underline the key words in the question.

> Choose *two* stories from **Opening Worlds** which you find both <u>moving</u> and <u>amusing</u>. <u>How do the writers</u> of each story arouse these responses in you? Remember to support your ideas with <u>details</u> from the texts.

Decide what the key words mean and think about what you are being asked to comment on:

- moving – touching my feelings (of anger, sadness, admiration)
- amusing – making me smile, funny
- how ... the writers – the writers' methods
- detail – references to the stories, quotations.

> ⚠ **Remember**
>
> Planning helps you think up and sort out your ideas and improves the structure and focus of your essays.

> 🔅 **Top tip**
>
> It can help to put the question to yourself in different ways, for example:
> - in what ways do the writers produce emotion and humour
> - what makes the stories both touching and funny?

b Brainstorm ideas and make a few notes for each of your two parents. Jot down some reminders about textual details and quotations you could use to support these points. For example:

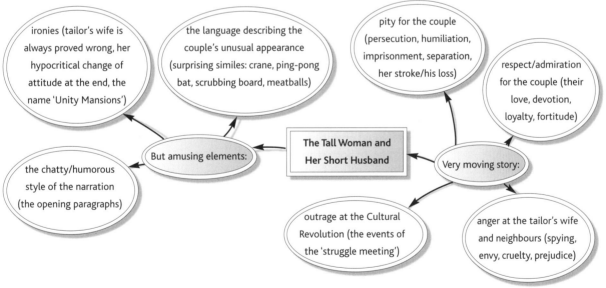

> 🔅 **Top tip**
>
> Use your plan to keep your answer on track.

Do a similar planning brainstorm for **Two Kinds**.

c Working from the brainstorms, decide how you would order the points. Give each point a number according to the order in which you would write about them. Discuss and compare your ideas with a partner.

! Remember

An introduction shows the examiner your overall approach and guides them into what you think about the stories.

🔆 Top tip

Keep introductions brief and clear; leave the detail to the main part of your answer.

4 Writing your answer

a Opening paragraph

Write your opening paragraph, using the following guidelines. First, introduce both of your chosen stories. Then in one or two sentences suggest general reasons for finding them moving and amusing, although not in any detail yet, but using the key words from the question.

b Following paragraphs

Use the following guidelines to write the main part of your answer.

✔ Keep the question in view and in mind throughout.

✔ Follow your plan of the points you are going to make and the order in which you are going to deal with them.

✔ Start each new paragraph with a point which clearly relates to the question.

✔ Use the writers' names and focus on the approaches they use rather than just telling the story.

✔ Use the three-point formula: Respond – Quote – Comment.

✔ Devote an equal amount of time and space to each story so that you produce a balanced answer.

✔ Show your awareness of links or differences between the two stories so that you avoid the impression of writing two different essays.

🔆 Top tips

- Check that your 'comments' are the longest parts of your paragraphs. If they aren't, spend more time developing your ideas.
- Make sure your 'comment' is focused on details such as the language which shows how the writer suggests ideas, and is not just a repeat of your 'respond' point. Try focusing on one or two words from your quotation and broaden out your comments from there.
- It's better to say a lot about a little, not the other way round. You cannot say everything that could be said about the stories, so aim to write about two or three things in detail.

c Final paragraph

Write your conclusion to the question using the guidelines below.

✔ Refer to both stories.

✔ Try to offer a fresh perspective so you are not just summing up and repeating yourself.

5 Checking your answer

Errors cost marks so it is worth taking the time to check:

✔ written expression

✔ spelling of the names of the writers and the characters

✔ other slips of the pen such as punctuation problems or words missed out

Finally, add any afterthoughts that occur to you as you read through to the end of the answer and indicate clearly, using an asterisk, numbers or letters, where they should be included.

Looking at candidates' answers

Complete sample answer

Read the following full answer to this question and decide on its strengths and weaknesses. What grade would you give it?

Aysha

'The Tall Woman and Her Short Husband' appears to be humorous at first. Ji-Cai uses many similies in her description of Mrs Tall and Mr Short. They conjure up interesting yet surreal and funny images, including 'like a crane over chickens' and a 'rubber roly-poly'. Not only are their individual descriptions funny but they are the complete opposite of each other and the children in the street give the funny image of them as 'Long carrying pole, big, low stool'. Mrs Tall and Mr Short aren't doing anything out of the ordinary, but because of their size they are outcast and ridiculed. We sympathise with them and feel sorry for what they have to put up with.

The tailor's wife is a character we love to hate. Although she is doing nothing legally wrong she is morally trespassing into the privacy and personal lives of two innocent people which makes us angry. She is described at the struggle meeting as 'full of self-importance and much fatter than before' and the unnecessary comment on her size brings a comic line and makes the reader feel good.

We start to feel even more sympathy towards the couple in the struggle meeting especially as Mr Short is 'threatened, beaten up, put under all kinds of pressure.' It is frustrating because we all know they have done nothing wrong. Mr Short and Mrs Tall are repeatedly humiliated, 'This wretch is too small' he is treated like a child and discriminated against because of his size. As the pressure builds up so does the suspense. To add to this tense atmosphere the tailor's wife shouts accusations at the couple and calls Mr Short a 'wretch – a broken reed'. We are irritated and frustrated by the fact that the couple don't fight back but we look up to them that after all they've been through, they don't stoop to that level.

As Mrs Tall gets back to her life we feel suspense to whether or not Mr Short will return, and at the line 'At the sound of his voice she sprang up to stare at him' the suspense is ripe. We feel the flood of emotions that passes between the two. After Mrs Tall's accident the impression of the love and devotion between the two is so strong that even the neighbours are 'touched by it' and the neighbours represent how the reader feels here.

'Two Kinds' is another story which seems humorous at first. Amy Tan describes things from the point of view of the young girl like Old Lady Chong 'had this peculiar smell like a baby that had done something in its pants' and it is funny that her piano teacher is deaf. It becomes very sad though that the mother puts so much pressure on the daughter that she feels she is a disappointment and only begins to understand her mother at the end after she is dead.

Remember

It's ok if your ideas about the stories are different from those here. The examiner is genuinely interested in what you think, not expecting one 'right' answer.

Strengths

✔ Good focus on the wording of the question (humorous, funny, writers' names, various emotional responses).
✔ Some awareness of the writers and their techniques (similes, images, descriptions, building suspense, point of view).
✔ Good variety of ways in which **The Tall Wife and Her Short Husband** is moving (sympathy, hatred, frustration, tension, irritation, respect, sadness, 'flood of emotions').
✔ Makes an attempt to link the two stories ('another story which seems humorous at first').
✔ Some well-selected references and quotations (the examples of similes, the final reaction of the neighbours, the young girl's view of Mrs Chong).
✔ Quotations are usually well integrated into the sentence ('even the neighbours are "touched by it"').
✔ Good vocabulary including some technical terms (similes, surreal, images, 'morally trespassing', 'discriminated against', suspense, point of view).
✔ Generally clear and accurate expression.

Weaknesses

✔ No opening paragraph introducing both stories – just dives into the first story.
✔ No concluding paragraph referring to both stories.
✔ Badly unbalanced. Only produces one rather rushed (but quite perceptive) final paragraph on the second story. Either the time planning has gone badly wrong or one story is much more familiar than the other.
✔ Some ideas not explained clearly or developed fully (the point about the size of the tailor's wife, the reasons why Mr Short is discriminated against, the final idea about **Two Kinds**).
✔ Some errors ('similies', 'outcast') and some quotations not fitting smoothly into sentences ('This wretch is too small').

Because of its unbalanced nature this is a difficult script to mark but Aysha was given a Band 3 mark for her answer which would bring her a Grade B overall. The section on **Two Kinds**, though brief, displayed enough insight and understanding to keep her in Band 3, but a more balanced answer could have taken her into Band 2 and a Grade A overall.

 Extension

Try this additional question: Explore the ways in which Nadine Gordimer and Ruth Prawer Jhabvala present conflicts between a husband and wife brought about by clashing cultures (in The Train from Rhodesia and The Young Couple).

Foundation Tier, Question 3

OPENING WORLDS

Tackling the question

Write about *two* stories from **Opening Worlds** in which different ways of life are brought into conflict. You should consider:
- who or what you think is to blame for the conflicts
- how the writing brings the conflicts alive for you.

 1 Choosing your question

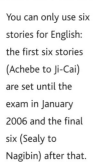 **! Remember**

You will lose marks if you don't answer the question fully or if you can't apply the question to the texts.

As you skim the story titles (six for English) on the Contents page of **Opening Worlds**, ask yourself:
- do conflicts between different ways of life spring to mind
- does my story concept map (see page 80) include 'culture clashes'?

If you keep answering 'no', don't choose this question. If you keep answering 'yes' to most of the above, go on to choose your stories. The question itself is not designed to trick or trap you and the wording is fairly straightforward. There is a clear subject area ('conflicting ways of life') which is probably one which you have thought about in relation to many of these stories. There are two clearly defined bullet points to tackle (on 'blame' and 'writing').

2 Choosing your stories

! Remember

You can only use six stories for English: the first six stories (Achebe to Ji-Cai) are set until the exam in January 2006 and the final six (Sealy to Nagibin) after that.

To find the best stories for you to answer the question, ask yourself:
- which stories can you use for English , rather than English Literature
- of the six, how many of these stories present conflicting ways of life
- of the six, how many stories could stimulate a discussion of 'blame'?

So, it remains a wide choice of six stories and you can narrow it down by deciding on the stories, conflicts and characters which have made the strongest impression on you. Let's go for **Dead Men's Path** and **Snapshots of a Wedding** which both present conflicts between traditional and more modern ways of life.

3 Planning your answer

You need to make a quick outline plan to help you structure your ideas.

a Underline the key words in the question.

Write about *two* stories from **Opening Worlds** in which <u>different ways of life</u> are brought into <u>conflict</u>. You should consider:
- <u>who or what</u> you think is to <u>blame</u> for the conflicts and
- how the <u>writing</u> brings the conflicts <u>alive for you</u>.

It can help to put the question to yourself in different ways, for example:

• which characters or circumstances bring about the disagreements or contrasting beliefs?

• which bits of the writing make me react more strongly to the disagreements and why?

Decide what the key words mean and think about what you are being asked to comment on:

• different ways of life – beliefs, attitudes, values, culture
• conflict – disagreement, falling-out, problems, clashing
• who/what – characters, situation, circumstances
• blame – cause, responsibility
• writing – quotations showing how the writers build up the conflict
• alive for you – the question is addressed to you, so pick out examples of the writing which move you and explain why.

b Brainstorm ideas and make a few notes for each of your two stories. Jot down some reminders about textual details and quotations you could use to support these points. For example:

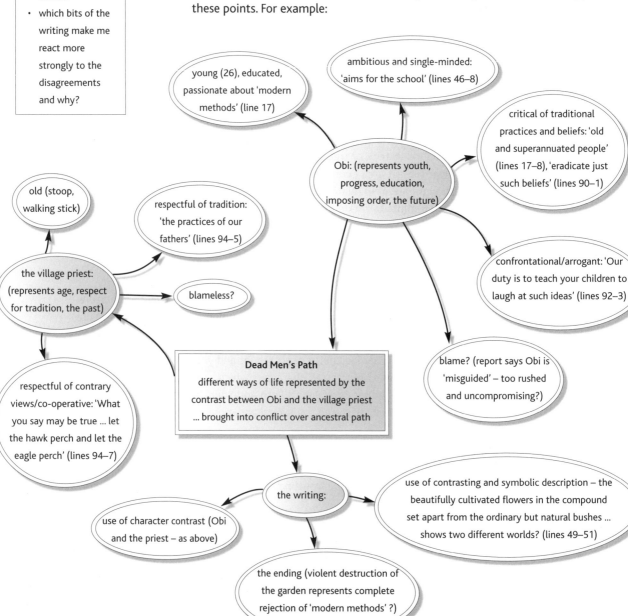

young (26), educated, passionate about 'modern methods' (line 17)

ambitious and single-minded: 'aims for the school' (lines 46–8)

critical of traditional practices and beliefs: 'old and superannuated people' (lines 17–8), 'eradicate just such beliefs' (lines 90–1)

Obi: (represents youth, progress, education, imposing order, the future)

old (stoop, walking stick)

respectful of tradition: 'the practices of our fathers' (lines 94–5)

the village priest: (represents age, respect for tradition, the past)

blameless?

confrontational/arrogant: 'Our duty is to teach your children to laugh at such ideas' (lines 92–3)

respectful of contrary views/co-operative: 'What you say may be true ... let the hawk perch and let the eagle perch' (lines 94–7)

blame? (report says Obi is 'misguided' – too rushed and uncompromising?)

Dead Men's Path
different ways of life represented by the contrast between Obi and the village priest ... brought into conflict over ancestral path

use of contrasting and symbolic description – the beautifully cultivated flowers in the compound set apart from the ordinary but natural bushes ... shows two different worlds? (lines 49–51)

the writing:

use of character contrast (Obi and the priest – as above)

the ending (violent destruction of the garden represents complete rejection of 'modern methods' ?)

Do a similar planning brainstorm for **Snapshots of a Wedding**.

c   Working from the brainstorms, decide how you would order the points dealing
with each story in turn. Number each point according to the order in which
you would write about them. Discuss and compare your ideas with a partner.

💡 Top tips

- Use your plan to keep your answer on track.
- You must tackle both bullet points in the question but don't deal with each bullet point for each
  story separately, which would risk repeating yourself and making your comments on the
  language seem separate to the theme. Instead, focus closely on the writing while you are
  tackling the idea of blame.

4 Writing your answer

a   **Opening paragraph**

First, introduce both of your chosen stories and their conflicts. Then in one or
two sentences suggest general reasons for blame, although not in any detail
yet, but using the key words from the question. Which of the following
candidates do you think gets off to the best start?

Hanif

In 'Snapshots of a Wedding' I blame Neo for
the conflict because she looks down on her
family and shows them no respect.

Wesley

In 'Dead Men's Path' the story begins
when Michael Obi is made headmaster of
the school.

Emily

'Educated as he was Kegoletile seemed to go
through a secret conflict ...'

Lucy

Both 'Dead Men's Path' and 'Snapshots of a
Wedding' present conflicts between new and
old ways of life.

Emma

The two stories I have chosen are 'Dead Men's
Path' and 'Snapshots of a Wedding'.

And the winner is ... Lucy! Hanif makes a good point but is already reaching a
conclusion in his first sentence rather than introducing the conflicts in both stories.
Wesley begins by telling the story rather than by focusing on the question. Emily
begins with a quotation – quite a good, relevant quotation but she doesn't make a
point first so the quotation will make no real sense to the examiner.

In fact, it's not a good idea to quote in your introductory paragraph. Use lots of quotations in the main part of your answer as you develop your points. Emma announces the stories she has chosen but doesn't say anything about them – and so is wasting valuable time.

Here is the whole of Lucy's introductory paragraph.

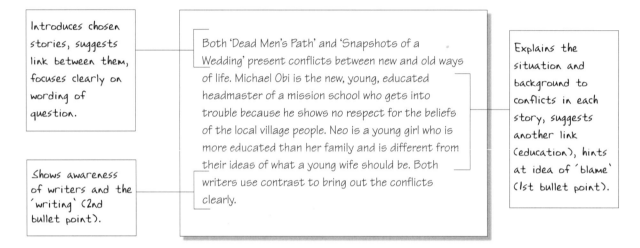

Introduces chosen stories, suggests link between them, focuses clearly on wording of question.

Shows awareness of writers and the 'writing' (2nd bullet point).

Both 'Dead Men's Path' and 'Snapshots of a Wedding' present conflicts between new and old ways of life. Michael Obi is the new, young, educated headmaster of a mission school who gets into trouble because he shows no respect for the beliefs of the local village people. Neo is a young girl who is more educated than her family and is different from their ideas of what a young wife should be. Both writers use contrast to bring out the conflicts clearly.

Explains the situation and background to conflicts in each story, suggests another link (education), hints at idea of 'blame' (1st bullet point).

b Following paragraphs

Use the following guidelines to write the main part of your answer.

✔ Keep the question in view and in mind throughout.

✔ Follow your plan of the points you are going to make and the order in which you are going to deal with them.

✔ Start each new paragraph with a point which clearly relates to the question.

✔ Use the writers' names and focus on the approaches they use rather than just telling the story.

✔ Use the three-point formula: Respond – Quote – Comment.

✔ Devote an equal amount of time and space to each story so that you produce a balanced answer.

✔ Show your awareness of links or differences between the two stories so that you avoid the impression of writing two different essays.

Top tips

Keep introductions brief and clear; leave the detail to the main part of your answer.

c   **Final paragraph**

Write your conclusion to the question using the guidelines below.

✔   Refer to both stories.

✔   Try to offer a fresh perspective so you are not just summing up and repeating yourself.

 5 Checking your answer

Errors cost marks so it is worth taking the time to check:

✔   written expression

✔   spelling of the names of the writers and the characters

✔   other slips of the pen such as punctuation problems or words missed out

Finally, add any afterthoughts that occur to you as you read through to the end of the answer and indicate clearly, using an asterisk, numbers or letters, where they should be included.

 Top tips

- Check that your 'comments' are the longest parts of your paragraphs. If they aren't, spend more time developing your ideas.
- Make sure your 'comment' is focused on details of the language which show how the writer suggests ideas, and is not just a repeat of your 'respond' point. Try focusing on one or two words from your quotation and broaden out your comments from there.
- It's better to say a lot about a little, not the other way round. You cannot say everything that could be said about the stories, so aim to write about two or three things in detail.

Looking at candidates' answers

Two complete sample answers

Read the two full answers to this question on page 122. Think about their strengths (indicated by the examiner with a number) and weaknesses, and about the kind of grade which you might give them.

Opening sentence is relevant and responds to two different conflicts.

2nd sentence responds more fully to Neo as a possible cause of conflict (relevance – 'blame').

Responds relevantly to the conflict in 2nd story; uses a textual detail (the footpath).

As with 1st story responds more fully to the conflict and to Obi as a possible cause (relevance – 'blame').

Susi

In 'Snapshots of a Wedding' the conflicts are between Neo and her family and between Mathata and Neo. It all comes down to the fact that Neo has got an education and is therefore seen as smug and superior. In 'Dead Men's Path' the conflict is about the little traditional footpath from the village to the burial place. Michael Obi, the new headmaster brings about the conflict by trying to change things.

It's difficult to tell whether Neo really is so smug and superior or if it is more the way her family and her society look upon a woman who has chosen a more modern way of life. **1** Although words like 'familiar careless disrespect' and 'haughty, **2** arrogant ways' crop up for Neo, you can't help wondering whether the writer shares the opinions of the family. **3** Mathata is described differently as ' a pretty girl with black eyes like stars' and 'always smiling and happy'. **4** She is not educated but she is more popular than Neo and much more like a traditional woman of that society as if it's better for a woman not to get too full of herself. **5**

Michael Obi tries to improve the school to more modern standards but he doesn't **6** listen to the village priest and simply says about it 'Dead men do not require footpaths' . When he shuts it down and a woman dies in childbirth, the traditional villagers take revenge. His plans are in 'ruins' at the end because he shows no **7** respect for local customs and comes across (like Neo) as arrogant. **8**

Both of the conflicts seem to be not just about people but about trying to break from tradition and trying something new. **9** And a conflict arises between tradition and modernisation. Perhaps the villagers and Neo's family are partly to blame because they are stuck in their ways **10** but the writing in both stories puts Neo and Michael Obi across as too full of importance. **11**

Ed

In the story of 'Dead Man's Path' it is obvious to me that the main conflict is due to the headmasters arrogance of the situation. **1** It is not ideal for the path to be there however he was warned of what might come by the priest and fellow colleges. **2** If respect for other peoples ways of life was taken into consideration then the problem would never of come about. **3** I think that the way that the story is written takes a sympathetic view from both sides. **4**

In the story 'Snapshots of a Wedding' the conflict is brought about by peoples beleived status in education and wealth. **5** Neo thinks shes better and this leads to jealousy, spite and maybe even hatred. **6** The writing makes the conflict seem very real. **7** It is something I can relate to in life, especially in education. The conflict was brought to life by being able to compare their lifestyles with my own.

Strengths

Examiners always start by looking for things to reward – by focusing on the strengths. Look at the five comments on Susi's first paragraph. Now look at the rest of the places in both Susi's and Ed's work where the examiner has indicated there is another strength and write out what the comment should be.

Weaknesses

The comments below apply to one of the answers. Which one? Look back at that answer and try to work out exactly what the examiner means.

- Very little textual detail - no direct quotation and therefore no evaluation of the writing.
- Limited range of response – rather brief.
- Reads like a long introduction and never gets to the textual detail.
- Response often vague and unexplained – personal and interesting, but not always saying anything relevant about the stories.
- Some problems of expression – of clarity, spelling, sentence endings and use of the apostrophe.

Examiner's comments

Susi

Fine opening paragraph. Grapples with different views of Neo in paragraph two and shows awareness of the writer. Selects quotations well and fits them into her sentences. Clear understanding of the conflicts in both stories and a balanced view of the idea of blame in the concluding paragraph. Links Neo and Obi cleverly ('arrogant'). Well-planned. Accurately and crisply expressed. Ideas not always fully developed (the comment about Mathata's name) or supported by references to the text (the family and the villagers being stuck in their ways). Not much close attention to the second bullet (the writing) - aware of the contrast between Mathata and Neo, for instance, but doesn't really comment on how the writing brings this out. Nevertheless shows 'clear sustained understanding' and makes 'relevant references to the texts'. Susi is working towards a Grade B overall if she keeps up this standard of work and she could certainly manage a Higher Tier paper. However, because this is Foundation Tier the highest she can be awarded is Grade C.

Ed

Understands the conflicts in both stories and responds directly to the wording of the question. Some strong personal response to the idea of 'blame'. Suggests understanding Achebe's 'sympathetic' view. However there are many weaknesses (see above). This candidate is underachieving simply because he doesn't use the texts. His ideas suggest that he is capable of achieving a high grade, but the lack of textual detail would keep him at Grade E level here.

Foundation Tier, Question 4
OPENING WORLDS

- English Lit: Unit 2
- 45 mins to answer
- Choice of 3 questions
- Worth 25% of mark

Tackling the question

Read the following extract (lines 133–94) from **Leela's Friend** and then answer the question below (in the exam the extract would be printed on the exam paper).

What do you find unfair about the treatment of Sidda in **Leela's Friend** and the treatment of a character in *one other* story from this collection. How do R. K. Narayan and the other writer you have chosen make you side with the victims of the unfair treatment?

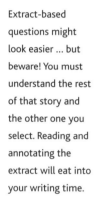

! Remember

Extract-based questions might look easier ... but beware! You must understand the rest of that story and the other one you select. Reading and annotating the extract will eat into your writing time.

 ## 1 Choosing your question

As you skim the extract in the question, ask yourself:
- does this extract seem familiar
- can I see the 'unjust treatment' of a clear 'victim'
- am I familiar with the whole of **Leela's Friend**, not just this extract?

As you skim the story titles on the Contents page of **Opening Worlds**, ask yourself:
- do other examples of 'unjust treatment' spring to mind?
- does my story concept map (see page 80) include 'unfairness or injustice' or a similar theme
- have I tackled a similar question as part of my revision?

If you keep answering 'no', don't choose this question. If you keep answering 'yes' to most of the above, go on to choose your other story and victims.

2 Choosing your stories

To find the best second story to answer the question , ask yourself:
- how many stories present victims of *clearly* unjust treatment
- of those six, how many stories make me side with the victim(s)
- of the six, how many stories present the unjust treatment and the victim(s) fully enough for me to build up a solid answer?

So, you might narrow it down to the following choices:
- Nak in **The Gold-Legged Frog**
- Mrs Tall and Mr Short in **The Tall Woman and Her Short Husband**
- Clement in **The Pieces of Silver**
- Bolan in **The Red Ball**
- Savushkin in **The Winter Oak**
- and Sidda in **Leela's Friend** which you *have* to include.

The examiners would be happy with other choices as well. You could shape good arguments about the unfairness of the racially divided society in **The Train from Rhodesia** or the way the mother brings up her daughter in **Two Kinds**, or the treatment of Ravi in **Games at Twilight** for example, but the six stories listed above probably provide the most clear-cut examples.

Top tip

It can help to put the question to yourself in different ways, for example:

• what is unjust about the treatment of the characters?

• how do the writers make me feel sorry for the 'victim' characters?

• what makes me share the feelings of the 'victims'?

3 Planning your answer

6 MINS

You need to make a quick outline plan to help you structure your ideas.

a Underline the key words in the question.

> What do you find <u>unfair</u> about the <u>treatment</u> of Sidda in **Leela's Friend** and the treatment of a character in *one other* story from this collection. <u>How</u> do R. K. Narayan and the other writer you have chosen make you <u>side with</u> the <u>victims</u> of the unfair treatment?

Decide what the key words mean and think about what you are being asked to comment on:

• unfair treatment – unjust handling, victimisation, cruelty
• how – the writers' methods
• side with – feel for, pity, identify with, support
• victims – the characters who are unjustly treated.

b Start by making use of the extract from **Leela's Friend** printed on the exam paper. Pick out examples which highlight Sidda's harsh treatment and make you feel sorry for him, and add brief comments. The first part has been done as an example.

Two officers – bullying, overpowering.

Leela (like the reader) sees Sidda as a patient and devoted friend.

Prejudiced adult view (contrasts with Leela's) – they see Sidda as a thief and traitor (no evidence).

Sidda – suffering, humiliated and defenceless (bowed/feebly/ looking at ground).

Four days later, just as Father was coming home from the office, <u>a police inspector and a constable</u> brought in Sidda. Sidda stood with <u>bowed head</u>. Leela was <u>overjoyed</u>. 'Sidda! Sidda!' she cried, and ran down the steps to meet him.

'Don't go near him,' the inspector said, stopping her.

'Why not?'

'He is a <u>thief</u>. He has taken away your gold chain.'

'Let him. I will have a new chain,' Leela said, and all of them laughed. And then Mr Sivasanker spoke to Sidda; and then his wife addressed him with a few words on his <u>treachery</u>. They then asked him where he had put the chain.

'I have not taken it,' Sidda said <u>feebly</u>, <u>looking at the ground</u>.

c Brainstorm some ideas and make a few notes for your second story. Jot down some reminders about textual details and quotations you could use to support these points. The following example is on **The Pieces of Silver**.

Clement is shamed in front of the school

he is forced to produce money even though his family is poor and the teachers are well-off (irony!)

characterisation – Clement's teacher, Chase, is presented as a bully who enjoys humiliating the boys (and detail)

Clement
what is unfair about Clement's treatment at school and how does Sealy present this unfairness and get us on Clement's side?

use of detailed description – of Clement's home (contrasted with Mr Megahey's), of their meal and of his mother's physical appearance, shows their poverty and wins sympathy (and detail)

use of contrast – the cold-hearted nastiness of Chase is set against the warmth and kindness of Clement's sister, Evelina (and detail)

> **! Remember**
>
> Planning helps you think up and sort out your ideas and improves the structure and focus of your essays.

> **💡 Top tip**
>
> Use your plan to keep your answer on track.

d Now decide how you would order the points dealing with each story in turn. Give each point a number according to the order in which you would write about them. Discuss and compare your ideas with a partner.

> **! Remember**
>
> An introduction shows the examiner your overall approach and guides them into what you think about the stories.

4 Writing your answer
25 MINS

a **Opening paragraph**
If your second story was **The Pieces of Silver**, you might first introduce the unfair treatment of both Sidda and Clement. In one or two sentences suggest ways the writers bring out the unfairness and make you side with Sidda and Clement. Do not go into detail yet, but use key words from the question.

b **Following paragraphs**
Use the guidelines given on page 114 to write the main part of your answer.

Read the following extracts taken from the middle sections of two candidates' answers and decide who you think is likely to be given a higher mark.

Lee

Sealy describes the cruel treatment of Clement in great detail. Chase makes him a 'laughing-stock' in front of the whole school just because he's too poor to hand his money in. He scrawls an X on his forehead and makes him recite threatening him with his cane. You can tell how upset Clement is because his eyes are 'downcast' like Sidda's in the other story and his voice is choked. He is also described as 'shabby and barefoot' which shows how poor he is and that he can't afford the money. This all shows the unfairness and makes me side with Clement against Chase.

Sara

When the day came that Sidda was accused of stealing Leela's chain he panicked and ran away until the police inspector brought him back. When Leela saw him she ran to him with joy wanting to be with him like the times before. But everyone stopped her from going near him but she responded with 'Let him. I will have a new chain.' As Sidda stood there his only hope was Leela who once had a caring trust with him. 'Oh policeman, leave him alone. I want to play with him.' The inspector kept telling the girl he was a thief but she didn't care she wanted Sidda back. They made a deal with Sidda to let him off if he returned the chain but Leela finally admits something which she never said before. 'Leave him alone he hasn't taken the chain.' Leela finally admits to putting the chain in the tamarind pot.

Examiner's comments

<u>Relevance/response</u>. The key difference between these two answers is clear in their opening sentences. Lee begins his paragraph with a point which tackles the question (how) directly and goes on to look at the effect of Sealy's descriptions. Sara begins by re-telling the story rather than by making a point and never really answers the question directly. She leaves it to the examiner to work out what is unjust and why we should side with Sidda and never really states her own view on this. Lee keeps an eye on the question and uses the key words ('unfairness', 'side with') very sensibly.

<u>Textual detail/evaluation</u>. Sara uses quotations from the extract but they are rather long and she doesn't comment on them. She seems slightly confused about what Leela actually admits to. Lee selects brief quotations, fits them into his sentences and tries to bring out their importance with his commentary. He makes an excellent link between the two stories and he keeps the writer in view. Sara obviously feels the unfairness of the situation and knows the story but, unlike Lee, she doesn't make her personal response very clear.

<u>Expression</u>. Sara has some difficulties with sentence boundaries, but Lee's expression is clear and accurate. He writes about the story in the present tense ('describes', 'makes', 'scrawls') whereas Sara mixes past and present ('came', 'panicked', 'admits'). It's better not to mix tenses and better to use the present.

<u>Overall comment</u>. Sara is working at a level here which could bring her a Grade D overall. Lee is working at a level which could take him to a Grade A overall and suggests that he could manage Higher Tier questions.

c   **Final paragraph**
Write your conclusion using the guidelines on page 114.

3 MINS **5 Checking your answer**

Errors cost marks so take the time to check the aspects listed on page 114.

Acknowledgements

The Publishers gratefully acknowledge the following for permission to reproduce copyright material. Whilst every effort has been made to trace the copyright holders, in cases where this has proved unsuccessful or if any have inadvertently been overlooked, the Publishers will be pleased to make the necessary arrangements a the first opportunity.

Extracts from 'Breakfast' by W. W. Gibson, from *Collected Poems* published by Macmillan. Reprinted with permission of Macmillan. Extract from 'Into my heart...' By A. E. Housman, reprinted by permission of The Society of Authors as the Literary Representative of the Estate of A. E. Housman. Extract from 'Clocks' and 'Babysitting' in full, by Gillian Clarke, from *Collected Poems* published by Carcanet Press Limited. Reprinted with permission of Carcanet Press Limited. Extracts from 'Poem' by Simon Armitage. Copyright © Simon Armitage. Reprinted by permission of David Godwin Associates. Extracts from 'Sonnet' by Edna St. Vincent Millay, from *Collected Poems* published by Carcanet Press Limited. Reprinted with permission of Carcanet Press Limited. Extracts from 'War Girls' by Jessie Pope from *Simple Rhymes for Stirring Times* published in 1916 by Arthur C. Pearson. Reprinted by permission of The Hamlyn Group. 'You're' by Sylvia Plath from *Collected Poems* by Sylvia Plath, published by Faber and Faber Limited. Extract from 'Mirror' by Sylivia Plath from from *Collected Poems* by Sylvia Plath, published by Faber and Faber Limited. Extract from 'Bedfellows' by Don Paterson, from *Nil Nil* published by Faber and Faber Limited. Extract from 'The Hare' by Selima Hill, from *Trembling Hearts in the Bodies of Dogs: New and Selected Poems* published by Bloodaxe Books 1994. Reprinted with permission of Bloodaxe Books Limited. Extract from 'The Target' by Ivor Gurney reprinted by permission of the Ivor Gurney Trust. Extract from 'The Hero' by Siegfried Sassoon Copyright © Siegfried Sassoon. Reprinted by kind permission of George Sassoon via Barbara Levy Literary Agency. Extract from 'Perhaps' is reprinted with the kind permission of her literary executors, Mark Bostridge and Rebecca Williams. Extracts from 'Defying Gravity' by Roger McGough, from *Defying Gravity* published by Penguin. Copyright © Roger McGough 1991, 1992. Reprinted with permission of Peters Fraser & Dunlop on behalf of Roger McGough. Extracts from 'Dead Man's Path' by Chinua Achebe published by Heinemann Educational. Reprinted by permission of REPP. Extract from 'Snapshots of a Wedding' by Bessie Head, published by Heinemann Educational. Reprinted by permission of REPP. Extracts from 'The Red Ball' by Ismith Khan, from *A Day in the Country* by Ismith Khan, published by Peepal Tree Press, 1994. Reprinted by permission of the publishers. Extracts from 'The Train to Rhodesia' by Nadine Gordimer from *Selected Stories* published by Jonathan Cape. Reprinted by permission of A. P. Watt Limited on behalf of Nadine Gordimer. Extracts from 'The Gold-Legged Frog' translated by Domern Garden, from *The Politician and Other Stories* published by Silkworm Books. Reprinted by permission of the author and Silkworm Books. Extracts from 'Two Kinds' by Amy Tan from *The Joy Luck Club* © 1989 Amy Tan. Reprinted by permission of Abner Stein. Extracts from 'The Tall woman and her Short Husband' by Feng Ji-Cai, translated to English by Gladys Yang © English Translation Gladys Young. Reprinted by permission of Yang Zhi (daughter of Gladys Young). Extracts from 'The Pieces of Silver' by Karl Sealy. Reprinted by kind permission of Beryl Sealy wife of the late Karl Sealy. Extracts from 'The Young Couple' by Ruth Prawer Jhabvala, from *A Stronger Climate* published by John Murray (Publishers) Limited. Reprinted by permission of the publishers. Extracts from 'Leela's Friend' by R. K. Narayan, from *Malguidi Days* first published in Great Britain by William Heinemann in 1982. Copyright © 1972, 1975, 1978, 1980, 1981, 1982 by R. K. Narayan. Reprinted by permission of The Random House Group Limited. Extracts from 'Games at Twilight' by Anita Desai, from *Games At Twilight* first published by Vintage. Copyright © Anita Desai 1978. Reproduced by permission of Rogers Coleridge & White Limited, 20 Powis Mews, London W11 1JN.